Demos is an independent think tank committed to radical thinking on the long-term problems facing the UK and other advanced industrial societies.

It aims to develop ideas – both theoretical and practical – to help shape the politics of the twenty first century, and to improve the breadth and quality of political debate.

Demos publishes books and a regular journal and undertakes substantial empirical and policy oriented research projects. Demos is a registered charity.

In all its work Demos brings together people from a wide range of backgrounds in business, academia, government, the voluntary sector and the media to share and cross-fertilise ideas and experiences.

For further information and
subscription details please contact:
Demos
The Mezzanine
Elizabeth House
39 York Road
London SE1 7NQ
email: mail@demos.co.uk
www.demos.co.uk

Surfing the Long Wave

Knowledge Entrepreneurship in Britain

Charles Leadbeater
and Kate Oakley

First published in 2001 by
Demos
The Mezzanine
Elizabeth House
39 York Road
London SE1 7NQ

ISBN 1 84180 045 7
Printed in Great Britain by Biddles Ltd
Design by Lindsay Nash

Contents

Acknowledgements

This report has taken almost three years to produce. We originally expected to publish it in 1999, after conducting a series of interviews with entrepreneurs and profiling the clusters and networks in which they worked. In some respects we are lucky we did not meet our original deadline. Had we done so we would have presented no more than a snapshot of our entrepreneurs at a moment in their career. As it was, we have had the opportunity to trace them through an extraordinarily uncertain, even tumultuous time.

Our research started in Spring 1998, well before the dot.com boom propelled a generation of young entrepreneurs into the limelight. For just over a year – early 1999 to the late spring of 2001 – it seemed as if entrepreneurs could build £1 billion businesses from scratch, armed with little more than a few good ideas. Since the onset of the dot.com crash, which started with the steep falls on the Nasdaq high-tech stock market in April 2001, a far more sober and cautious mood has descended upon financial markets, venture capitalists and many entrepreneurs. We have been able to trace a group of entrepreneurs through this upheaval. As a result we hope our findings will be both more interesting and more robust.

We have a large number of people to thank for their help with this project, which began with conversations with Sir Douglas Hague of Templeton College Oxford, who gave us the idea to look at knowledge entrepreneurs. Roger Baker, formerly of the Gatsby Charitable Foundation, and Michael Pattison, its director, have been very understanding when the project took longer than originally planned.

At Demos Tom Bentley has summoned up more patience than anyone should have to and Lindsay Nash has edited the text and designed the report with her customary professionalism. We should like to thank all the entrepreneurs who allowed us to interview them, sometimes several times. Between December 1999 and February 2001 Charles Leadbeater worked as an adviser to Atlas Venture, the venture capital fund, and learned an enormous amount about the funding and development of high growth entrepreneurial businesses. He would like to thank Chris Spray and the staff at Atlas Venture for their help. We have learned from many people, not least the entrepreneurs we interviewed as well as Peter Swann, David Teece, Charles Hill, John Gray and Fernando Flores.

1. Why entrepreneurship matters

This report aims to explode some of the myths that cloud our understanding of entrepreneurship, confuse our attitudes towards it and provide misleading guides for policies to promote it.

Put very crudely, entrepreneurship is an activity in which a partnership or team of people, combining different skills, identify an opportunity to create a new product or service and then mobilise the resources, both financial and human, to realise the idea.

This report, based on interviews over the past three years with tens of British entrepreneurs, makes three main claims about the role of entrepreneurship in modern society.

Collaborative entrepreneurship

Entrepreneurship is taking new forms: it is increasingly less individualistic and more collaborative.

The traditional view is that an entrepreneur is either a struggling small businessman or a lone hero with the charismatic qualities to take risks and persuade others to back their judgement: Anita Roddick, Alan Sugar or Richard Branson, for example. Our research shows that this stereotype is increasingly misleading.

While entrepreneurs are often be lone mavericks, *entrepreneurship* is a far more structured, often team-based activity. Public policy should be less concerned with creating incentives for lone entrepreneurs and more concerned with promoting the conditions for successful entrepreneurship as an activity. Entrepreneurship succeeds by pulling together the different skills and know-how needed to turn an idea into a business, product or service.

Successful entrepreneurial organisations never depend on a single individual: they are the creations of partnerships and teams of people who bring together the technical, commercial, marketing and financial skills needed to turn an idea into a business. An individual entrepreneur may kick off the process by identifying the opportunity. In some cases the individual entrepreneur can go on to lead the team. However often the founder entrepreneur plays a critical role only at the start of what turns out to be a very long process of entrepreneurship involving trial, error, learning and discovery.

Several conclusions follow from this recognition that entrepreneurship is the preserve of partnerships and teams rather than individuals.

- Entrepreneurs are highly individualistic. But to succeed they also have to be highly collaborative to pull together the other people they need to realise an idea.

- Founder entrepreneurs often spot an opportunity in a flash of insight and move to exploit their ideas far more quickly than a large organisation would. That is why entrepreneurship is associated with agility. The truth, however, is that entrepreneurship is a very time-consuming activity that requires great persistence. Invariably is takes several years to combine the ingredients for a successful business. The dot.com boom of the late 1990s created the impression that entrepreneurs could make quick returns. Most successful entrepreneurs have to wait several years for their ideas to come to fruition.

- Entrepreneurs cannot afford to be loners. The idea of the entrepreneur as a lone inventor is utterly misleading. Entrepreneurs work in partnerships, networks and clusters, to acquire ideas, information, contacts, relationships and resources. Entrepreneurs are intensely social.

- Entrepreneurs are motivated by profit but also by a sense of achievement and independence in being able to create an organisation with its own work-style, philosophy and products. The creative and independent impulse behind entrepreneurship is at least as important as the financial and commercial impulse. The rise of entrepreneurship is as much a cultural and social phenomenon, an expression of the more independent values of a younger generation, as it is a reflection of the financial and economic calculations they make.

The entrepreneurial society

A widespread capacity for entrepreneurship is increasingly critical for a successful modern society.

Entrepreneurship is traditionally seen as an important tool for job creation, both through the growth of micro-businesses and self-employment, and through the creation of high-growth new businesses. Entrepreneurs are agents of change. By spotting new opportunities to use resources more effectively, they help to shift the economy's resources from areas of low growth into areas of high growth. This is why entrepreneurship is so vital to the flexibility and adaptability of open, market economies. However, the traditional focus on entrepreneurship as a source of job creation is too narrow. It underestimates the economic significance of entrepreneurship and ignores its social and cultural role.

In an innovation-driven economy, entrepreneurship takes on a much greater significance. First, entrepreneurship plays a vital role in innovation. Entrepreneurs excel at translating new ideas into products, services, businesses and organisations. In fast-moving industries where new ideas emerge rapidly, large companies are frequently less able to absorb, adapt and use ideas than smaller firms. The speed and spread of modern technologies of communications, computing, software and biotechnology means we are in a period of extraordinary entrepreneurial opportunity, especially in high-tech and scientific fields.

In industries such as computing and software, where new ideas emerge from many different sources – small companies and large as well as universities – people will disagree on the potential value of different ideas. Which will be the right way to incorporate computing power into clothing? Will open standards such as Linux triumph over Microsoft's Windows operating system? These disagreements are the breeding ground for entrepreneurs who believe they can spot opportunities that others have overlooked or ignored.

The more rapid and fragmented the nature of knowledge creation within an industry the more conducive it is for entrepreneurship. We are living through a period of heightened entrepreneurial activity in part because modern societies invest so much in scientific research and innovation. In industries where knowledge does not move so fast, for example more mature manufacturing industries or regulated industries such the law, there will be fewer new ideas, less doubt about the value of those ideas and thus fewer opportunities for entrepreneurship.

Second, entrepreneurs spur improvements in productivity by challenging incumbents in established markets. Entrepreneurial businesses exploit falling barriers to entry to attack entrenched incumbents: they contest once cosy markets. Barriers to entry are falling thanks to four main forces: deregulation in industries such as telecommunications and financial services, which has allowed in new entrants; globalisation, which has encouraged competition from developing regions in the world economy; the falling price of technology, which allows new entrants to enter markets with a much lower cost base than companies with established production lines; corporate strategies increasingly based on extending successful brands into new markets, which for example has allowed companies like Tesco, the retailer, to enter financial services.

Even if entrepreneurial challengers do not succeed, their entry into the market challenges incumbents to improve their performance. The value of entrepreneurship often shows up in the form of higher productivity in incumbent companies that have to fight off a challenge. While many "dot.coms" have failed, for example, they have spurred many large companies to invest in E-business solutions to make themselves more efficient and responsive to customers. Large companies increasingly need a capacity for entrepreneurship within their own ranks, to respond to these challenges.

Entrepreneurship does not matter just for economic reasons: it also brings enormous social benefits. A widespread capacity for entrepreneurship will increasingly be seen as a mark of a healthy society.

A society that seeks to foster entrepreneurship must foster the culture that feeds it: openness, meritocracy, democracy and adaptive institutions. Entrepreneurship will become more central to our society because more people are attracted to the independence and sense of achievement it provides. People are increasingly self-managing their careers rather than relying on a corporation to do it for them. The line between employment and self-employment is blurring. A widespread capacity for micro-entrepreneurship will be increasingly important to an adaptive economy.

Entrepreneurship thrives when people can think and act independently, qualities that are bred in open, democratic and pluralistic societies, with education systems that encourage young people to think creatively. An education system that encourages conformity and discourages independent initiative will not encourage entrepreneurship.

A society can only encourage entrepreneurship when it is open to people with talent, ideas and ambition who may come from outside the establishment. Often entrepreneurs have unconventional backgrounds: they are rebels, drop-outs and dissenters. Entrepreneurs frequently challenge vested interests. In doing so they can help to erode established concentrations of power. An entrepreneurial culture is one mark of an open society.

Entrepreneurship also promotes social mobility, especially for recent immigrants. The entrepreneurial openness of the US is one reason why it has attracted so much talent from around the world. Indian or Chinese immigrants created almost 3,000 high-tech companies in California in the 1990s. The more entrepreneurial an economy is the more it should create opportunities for immigrants and ethnic minorities, the more attractive it should be to mobile entrepreneurial talent and the better able it should be to sustain a multicultural society.

A healthy society needs entrepreneurial capacity to feed the learning, experimentation and renewal of the public sector as much as the private sector. The welfare state emerged not just from overarching public policy initiatives at the close of the Second World War, such as the Beveridge Plan and the 1944 Education Act. It also emerged from a string of entrepreneurial attempts to create new schools, hospitals and welfare schemes outside the ambit of the state, especially in the first half of the twentieth century. It was the combination of far-sighted policy making at the centre and entrepreneurial imagination at the grassroots that paved the way for the modern welfare state. In a society of rapid change, an entrepreneurial capacity within public services will be even more important.

All entrepreneurs, in whatever walk of life, are in the future business: they are attempting to chart new routes into the future for their business, organisation or industry. Entrepreneurs believe they can do something differently and in the process, if only in a small way, they change the way society works. As Charles Spinosa, Fernando Flores and Hubert Dreyfus put it in their book of the same title: entrepreneurs "disclose new worlds" that people did not realise might exist. David Harvey, the Marxist geographer, puts the same point a different way in his book *Places of Hope* when he argues that capitalism thrives not just on financial speculation but more fundamentally on a speculative capacity to dream up different futures.

This is why entrepreneurship is so vital to the health of society. Entrepreneurs help to navigate different possible routes into the future: different ways to communicate, entertain, learn, save, shop, trade, vote, treat disease or save the environment. Entrepreneurs create new ways forward. For any society that is a vital capacity.

An infrastructure for entrepreneurship

Entrepreneurship has become so central to modern society that its promotion can no longer be left to the chance emergence of charismatic individuals with special qualities. We need a far more systematic and comprehensive policy framework to spread entrepreneurial capacity across society.

Traditionally, entrepreneurship is covered by economic policy. Entrepreneurs are largely motivated by the pursuit of profit, the argument goes, so the main role of policy is to make it as easy as possible for entrepreneurs to start and grow a business, for example by reducing business regulations, and to make it as rewarding as possible for them by lowering taxes.

There are limits to how far public policy can influence the level of entrepreneurship in a society, which is deeply influenced by culture, attitudes towards risk and also practical issues such as the availability of finance. However, even within those limits, public policy can and should go substantially further in promoting a deeper, more widely distributed entrepreneurial culture in the UK. Since 1997 the Labour government has introduced a range of policies that touch on entrepreneurship, including relaxing some rules on stock options, encouraging universities to create spin-off businesses, promoting regional venture capital funds and encouraging pension funds to invest more in venture capital.

Our analysis shows that we need a more systematic and comprehensive approach that draws together economic and social policies, stretching from education through to business regulation and financial markets. As a part of that the machinery of government needs an overhaul, with a radical reorganisation of the main Whitehall department involved – the Department of Trade and Industry – and a new government-wide focus on entrepreneurship and innovation from the heart of government economic policy-making in the Treasury.

Central reorganisation needs to be accompanied by the creation of new institutions, such as a Knowledge Bank to help large companies finance promising developments in small companies. A stronger local and regional capacity for economic development will be vital as many of these issues can only be tackled close to the ground.

This policy framework should include these ingredients:

- Building entrepreneurial capacity through education and skills, attracting entrepreneurial talent from abroad and helping groups with relatively low entrepreneurial activity – women, employees over the age of 45 and ethnic minorities – to start businesses.
- Opening up entrepreneurial opportunity through a rigorous competition policy biased in favour of new entrants, including in the public sector and highly regulated sectors such as professional services
- Developing entrepreneurial hubs, networks and clusters, especially in regions with limited entrepreneurial activity, to help entrepreneurial teams to mobilise the resources they need to turn an idea into a business, including access to finance, people and corporate partnerships.
- Promoting entrepreneurship and innovation from within the public sector to encourage the creation of new models for public services from the ground up.
- Improving the recognition and rewards for entrepreneurship by further simplifying rules governing stock options in growing companies and through the launch of an annual National

Business Plan competition, akin to a Booker Prize for business, with different categories for school children, students and entrepreneurs over 50.

During a period of rapid change and disruption, entrepreneurs weave together the resources that make new products, services and ways of living a practical possibility for many people. Entrepreneurs are agents of change, pathfinders who help to chart our transition from one kind of society to another. Their contribution is not just in creating jobs or wealth. As William Gibson the science fiction writer put it: "The future is here, it's just not very widely distributed yet." Entrepreneurs, at their best, help create and distribute the future.

The research

The research for this report focused on a new breed of knowledge entrepreneurs who build their businesses almost entirely on the exploitation of ideas and know-how. Over three years we interviewed knowledge entrepreneurs in different fields at different stages of business development. (See the Appendix for a full list of those interviewed.) We interviewed and examined the case histories of :

- Eight scientific entrepreneurs who were running businesses based on formal scientific knowledge often derived from universities. These included Robin Saxby, chief executive of ARM, Edwin Moses of Oxford Assymetry, Paul Drayson of PowderJect, Andrew Rickman of Bookham Technologies and Danny Chapchal at Cambridge Display Technologies.
- Ten internet entrepreneurs, among them Brent Hooberman of Lastminute.com, Toby Rowland and Robert Norton, of Click Mango, Steve Bowbrick of WebMedia and Another.com.
- Seven computer games entrepreneurs, among them Jez San at Argonaut, Peter Molyneux at Lionhead and Ian Stewart, former head of the Gremlin group.
- Seven animation entrepreneurs among them David Sproxton, co-founder of Aardman animation, and several other leading British animators.
- In addition, we interviewed about fifteen entrepreneurs in cultural industries such as design, television and film, among them Daljit Singh, creative director and co-founder of Digit, the award winning design studio, and Simon Waterfall, creative director of Deepend, the web design company.

The aim of our research was not to profile these entrepreneurs, nor to explore their backgrounds and motivations. These entrepreneurs represent a new breed: they have built their businesses almost entirely on intangible assets such as know-how. Our aim was to examine what entrepreneurship amounts to in an economy in which the generation, application and exploitation of distinctive know-how is fast becoming the prime source of wealth creation.

2. The six stages of entrepreneurship

Paul Drayson could sense the potential as soon as the idea was explained to him. Patients could have a painless injection delivered by a device the size of a mobile telephone that sounded like something from Star Trek. A doctor would wave the device over the patient's arm to deliver a treatment in hundreds of particles so small that the patient would not notice them. The device is a PowderJect. The way it was developed exemplifies many aspects of how knowledge entrepreneurship works.

In 1992 Paul Drayson, a young entrepreneur who had developed and sold a couple of businesses in the food industry, quite by chance met Brian Bellhouse, a scientist at Oxford University who had the vision of the painless injection. Bellhouse and his colleague David Sarphie had been working with geneticists at Oxford to insert genetic material deep into plant cells using a high-powered gas-gun.

As the gun worked on plants, Bellhouse conjectured it would also work on humans. He and Sarphie loaded the gun with microscopic salt particles. Bellhouse put his hand in front of the gas jet. The salt flew at high speed into Bellhouse's hand yet he felt nothing. They had discovered a painless way to deliver medicines usually delivered by injections.

The two scientists only had a dim sense of their invention's commercial and medical potential. It was Bellhouse's daughter, Elspeth who saw the potential and persuaded them to patent their invention. She also insisted that they team up with an entrepreneur to develop the idea into a business, which is where Paul Drayson came in.

When Drayson arrived at Bellhouse's laboratory he did not find a hand-held device from Star Trek but a gas gun the size of a bazooka.

Drayson realised that the idea's potential would be made good only if they could mobilise and apply more resources. Drayson used his own funds to further develop the gun and to take out patents on powder injection techniques around the world. He spent nine months in negotiations with Oxford University over ownership of the intellectual property rights.

Drayson realised the key to the company was its intellectual property. Yet he also knew that strong patents on their own would not be enough. The PowderJect company would have neither the resources nor the skills to exploit the invention's potential to the full. He set out to form partnerships with companies that had the resources that PowderJect needed: technology, distribution, marketing, sales. PowderJect has formed partnerships with more than a dozen pharmaceutical companies, including Glaxo-Wellcome, Pfizer and Roche to develop treatments delivered by the PowderJect. To turn Bellhouse and Sarphie's bazooka into a hand-held device, Drayson signed a deal with BOC to manufacture tiny helium gas cylinders. PowderJect is not yet launched as a commercial product yet the company had a stock market valuation on its flotation in 1998 of more than £600 million.

PowderJect exemplifies many of the ingredients that make knowledge entrepreneurship a success.

First, the company is based upon distinctive know-how, the Bellhouse and Sarphie research, which took many years to develop and is very hard to imitate. Bellhouse began research on high-speed gases shortly after the Second World War.

Second, the inventors did not sense the opportunity the invention had created. That only came from the entrepreneurs, Bellhouse's daughter Elspeth and Paul Drayson (who subsequently married one another). It was only when the inventors teamed up with the entrepreneurs that the idea was turned into a business. PowerJect, like many other successful high-technology companies, is built on the partnership between science and entrepreneurs

Third, the raw knowledge at the core of the business had to be put into a form that could be protected but also replicated in the shape of a product. Bellhouse and Sarphie had created a generic technology: powder injection. Powderdject had to turn that into a product: something that could be used day in day out by doctors.

Fourth, to make that possible the team had to mobilise resources beyond its control: it had to form collaborative partnerships.

Fifth, they had to act confidently in the face of great uncertainty. PowderJect started as a very small company facing many larger competitors. Several times the team rejected offers to buy the business. Drayson had to recruit key staff from secure jobs in larger companies to join a fledgling venture. This required a potent mixture of confidence and flexibility, vision and pragmatism: confidence to punch above the company's weight, and flexibility to quickly change tactics when conditions changed.

Not all knowledge-based businesses go through exactly this cycle. PowderJect, like other science-based businesses, started with a technology and then found a market for it. Often businesses start the other way around: an entrepreneur senses an opportunity and finds the technology to realise it. Knowledge entrepreneurship cannot be reduced to a template, as the diversity of experiences in our case studies show.

Entrepreneurship is chaotic. Events rarely turn out as planned. Business plans are frequently rewritten. Chance, luck and serendipity play an enormous role. Peter Molyneux, one of Britain's most successful computer games entrepreneurs, stumbled into the industry almost by chance after persuading Commodore, the computer group, to give him and his partner some of its smartest machines. Jez San, the founder of Argonaut Software and ARC, which designs chips for games consoles, started his career by spending two years in his bedroom designing a computer game called Starglider that quite by chance became an enormous hit. Edwin Moses became chief executive of Oxford Assymetry, the biotechnology firm, as a removals firm was packing up his belonging to take him to a job in Chicago. Steve Bowbrick created one of the earliest successful British web design companies, WebMedia, only to see it fail. Bowbrick then spent the best part of a year looking for a new venture. He tried and rejected about five ideas before finally settling on his new venture, Another.com.

Experimentation, learning, failure and risk taking are vital to entrepreneurship. It cannot be reduced to a manageable process. However our research shows that knowledge entrepreneurship as an activity shares these fundamental characteristics:

- Successful knowledge entrepreneurship is a structured activity, not a flash of individual genius. Outsiders, advisers and intermediaries can play a crucial role in structuring this activity.
- Knowledge entrepreneurship builds in six stages: create, sense, package, mobilise, act and exit. A business can succeed or fail at any stage. All stages can be affected by policy makers to increase the chances that entrepreneurial venture will succeed.
- The basic unit of knowledge entrepreneurship is not the individual but partnerships and teams that combine the different skills needed to take a venture through these stages.
- These teams are often put together through social and business networks that are often animated by intermediaries, including investors such as venture capitalists, colleagues who worked together for large companies or universities acting as hubs.
- While entrepreneurs are more agile than larger companies it often takes several years for a idea to come to fruition. Persistence counts as much as agility.

The six stages of entrepreneurship

Create

Successful knowledge businesses are built on distinctive and valuable know-how that has a potential to create a new service or to improve productivity, which competitors will find it hard to imitate.

The importance of distinctive valuable knowledge is most obvious in science-based businesses such as CDT, PowderJect, Renovo and ARM, which were built on formal scientific knowledge developed over several years of non-commercial research. Yet this is only one kind of knowledge that can be deployed in a knowledge business. Steve Bowbrick's successful e-mail business Another.com was based on a sound knowledge of the internet and an eye for how to market a product virally by word of mouth. Jez San's Argonaut was built on the tacit, informal and untaught skills of computer games programmers. In creative businesses, such as Aardman animation, the knowledge is embedded in the creative processes and culture of the company.

Often entrepreneurs do not create new ideas, know-how or skills: they take ideas from one area and apply them to another. Entrepreneurs are inveterate borrowers, often abducting an idea or an experience from one area and applying it to another. The failure of many of the first wave of internet businesses – the dot.coms – was in part due to their lack of a really distinctive know-how. Often these companies were simply slightly quicker to understand how the internet could be applied to business than larger incumbents. Once the incumbents got up to speed many of the new entrants were squeezed out.

Sense
Knowledge businesses do not necessarily have to start with distinctive knowledge at the outset. Many knowledge based businesses start with a sense of the market opportunity and then put together the know-how needed to exploit it.

Entrepreneurs sense opportunities that others do not see. Entrepreneurship is not about simply being quick enough to exploit a market that everyone can see: the goldrush had nothing to do with entrepreneurship. The most impressive entrepreneurs see opportunities that most people overlook or doubt exist.

Entrepreneurs thrive amid a consensus of doubt and scepticism that holds other people back. They believe they are able to spot emerging trends from the fog of uncertainty that often surrounds new technologies and emerging markets. Armed with a minimum of information they can work out more quickly and confidently what is going on around them.

Timing is vital. Entrepreneurs can fail just as easily entering a market too early as entering too late. This was the fate of many first-wave internet businesses: they got to the market so quickly that it was not mature enough to support their businesses. Many suffered from first mover disadvantage rather than first mover advantage. Slower moving companies following in their wake were able to learn from their mistakes.

This ability to sense opportunity is sometimes the result of a flash of insight. It is rarely the product of formal market research. Entrepreneurs learn to sense opportunity in several ways:

- Entrepreneurs invest in trial and error. Steve Bowbrick, for example, drew up plans for five different companies before he hit upon the idea for Another.com with Joel Koerner. Through each attempt to create a business plan he learned a little more about what would and would not work.

- Entrepreneurs often have a confident and committed view of the world. They make up their minds rapidly because they have faith in their ability to make sense of the world. This confidence sometimes comes from their youth – the likes of Jez San, the teenage entrepreneur at Argonaut – and sometimes from great experience – the likes of Robin Saxby, the seasoned ex Motorola executive who played the role of elder statesman at ARM.
- Entrepreneurs often foster intelligence networks of friends, colleagues and partners through which they can share ideas, learn what competitors are doing and glean information about new opportunities. Sensing opportunity is as much a social activity as an analytic and intellectual one.

Knowledge-based businesses combine these first two ingredients: distinctive capability or know-how and a sense of an opportunity that others overlook.

Sometimes the knowledge at the core of the business and the sense of opportunity can be found in a single person. David Ferguson, the founder of Renovo, is a good example. Renovo is developing commercial products to prevent patients scarring after surgery or accidents. Ferguson is both the chief scientist behind Renovo and the most articulate exponent of the scale of its opportunity in world health markets. Ferguson's sense of the scale of the commercial opportunity for Renovo comes directly from his intimate knowledge of surgery and scarring.

However most often, as in the case of PowderJect, the sense of opportunity and the distinctive know-how come from different people whose talents are combined in a partnership.

An economy will create entrepreneurial knowledge-based businesses only where both knowledge and a sense of opportunity are in good supply. Investment in the knowledge base, not just in education but also through research and development, science and culture, has to be matched by creating open markets in which new entrants can challenge incumbents.

Package

It is not enough for a venture to have identified an opportunity and posses the distinctive and valuable know-how to exploit it. To be successful that know-how has to be packaged in a form the company can exploit. Brian Bellhouse and David Sarphie invented a generic technology, powder injection; Paul Drayson and Elspeth Bellhouse turned that into a product, a medical device.

The trick is to come up with a technology, business model, brand or service that competitors will find it hard to imitate but which the company itself can replicate and so spread to a large market. The product or service has to be simple for consumers to use; yet the knowledge underlying must be complex enough to make it difficult for competitors to imitate.

The best example of why this packaging matters is the case of Cambridge Display Technologies. CDT makes a new kind of screen for computers, televisions and mobile telephones, based on a plastic that can emit light, (Light Emitting Polymer or LEP.) CDT began life in 1989 with the chance discovery in a Cambridge physics laboratory, in work involving physicists and chemists, exploring the potential for polymers to act as semi-conductors. Jeremy Burroughs, a researcher, found that polymers glowed when subject to electricity at low voltage. With his supervisor, physics professor Dr Richard Friend, he founded CDT. The potential for LEP technology is enormous. LEP screens are simpler and cheaper to produce than existing screens; they do not need separate illumination; they can be viewed from any angle; they are extremely flexible and environmentally friendly.

Yet despite the promise of the technology, for most of the 1990s CDT struggled because it failed to turn a generic technology into a specific product with a market. CDT has recognised that alone it cannot develop the technology into a product; it needs to work with partners who can.

To make this transition from a basic technology to a specific product, the original inventor or founder entrepreneur has to be prepared to work with people who have applied know-how in manufacturing, distribution and marketing. This transition is not just a problem for science-based companies. In cultural and creative businesses, such as computer games and animation, the distinctive know-how of the creators has to be combined with the clout of distributors and publishers to create a successful business. Moving through this stage of the entrepreneurial process invariably involves expanding the team to draw in complementary business skills. That can often provoke conflict.

Mobilise

A company cannot to make the transition from simply having an idea to become a business with a product, without mobilising additional resources. Entrepreneurs excel at rallying money, people and resources to their cause. Knowledge entrepreneurs are ideas and purpose in search of assets and resources. Large companies are generally assets and resources in search of ideas and purpose.

Entrepreneurs have to be good at mobilising three kinds of asset: finance, people and partners.

● Finance

All entrepreneurial businesses need finance to grow. Capital markets and investors play a critical role in financing the risks that entrepreneurs take. The emergence of a new generation of entrepreneurial businesses in the UK in the past decade has been due in part to the emergence of a deeper and more sophisticated venture capital industry, which is now investing more in start-ups and new technologies. In the past two years many large companies, such as BT and Reuters, have created corporate venture funds to invest in new ideas inside and outside their businesses. A clutch of business incubators has been set up, such as Gorilla Park, BrainSpark and IdeasHub. Government policy has promoted the venture capital industry through regional venture capital funds and venture capital trusts.

None of the entrepreneurs we interviewed complained that it had been difficult to raise finance. Most started their businesses with a mixture of their own savings, sweat equity and bank loans, and then funded the business from their revenues. A few got funding from individual angel investors or formal government schemes, such as the Loan Guarantee Scheme. Finance still remains an issue for many small companies, especially those that are too small to attract venture capital but too large to be financed from bank overdrafts. Raising finance requires specific skills – in business planning, financial projections and negotiations with investors – which the originators of an idea or tech-nology often lack.

● *People*
Entrepreneurs have to be good at creating teams that mix different talents and ages. Often one problem that besets entrepreneurial busi-nesses is that they find it difficult to attract management talent from larger more established companies. One of the biggest constraints facing smaller companies is the difficulties they have in recruiting managers ready to work in an entrepreneurial environment.

● *Partnerships*
Small companies often come up with innovations that are only legit-imised when larger companies exploit them. Often smaller companies do not challenge large incumbents directly but find a profitable niche within an ecology of existing companies, supplying them with new ideas and services. Many of the most successful companies we examined worked in alliance with large partners. ARM has grown with Nokia, its main customer for semi-conductors. PowderJect relies on its alliance with pharmaceutical companies. Aardman was worked with larger distributors for its products.

To mobilise resources, entrepreneurial teams have to combine at least three qualities. First, they have to be good storytellers, to communicate the excitement of the project. Second, they need to be able to explain to investors the financial detail of business plans. Third, they need to be good negotiators and networkers to form the right partnerships and corporate alliances.

Act
Entrepreneurs act confidently in the face of uncertainties that put off other people. This requires a blend of confidence and flexibility, vision and opportunism.

Entrepreneurs have to have great confidence in the idea behind their business and its potential for growth. Especially when a company is small, the entrepreneur has to be able to communicate this vision to employees, investors and partners alike. That confidence rarely comes from having a detailed strategy or a well-developed business plan. It comes from a sense of commitment and self-belief in the project. This is something that often only the founder entrepreneur can provide.

Yet, as well as being committed, entrepreneurs have to be flexible and open in the way that they think about developing their business. As market conditions change, new competitors emerge and investor sentiment shifts, entrepreneurs have to be flexible enough to change tack. Internet and E-commerce companies, for example, such as NoHo Digital and Another.com have had to adapt and change their business models of where they would make their money from as the business has developed. NoHo was set up to exploit the CD-rom market that quickly collapsed. It then did a lot of work for Microsoft only to have the plug pulled on its main contract. It prospered in the late 1990s by becoming a web designer.

Frequently entrepreneurial businesses have to take opportunities, clients and investors as they present themselves. It is extremely rare for an entrepreneurial business to develop according to the original plan of the founders.

The group of entrepreneurs we studied have been through a huge amount of turmoil. Several of the companies changed hands, among them NoHo Digital, which was sold to WPP the advertising and marketing group; WIRE, the internet insurance specialist which was bought to the Willis Insurance group; and Oxford Assymetry, the biotechnology company, which was sold to Evotech. Eidos, the maker of the computer game Tomb Raider starring Lara Croft which at its peak was worth £12 a share, remains independent only after a series of failed merger talks and with its share price in May 2001 at £3 per share. A handful of the entrepreneurs went out of business altogether, among them Lesley Keen a leading computer games entrepreneur in Scotland and Robert Norton and Toby Rowland of Click Mango. Others such as Bookham Technologies and ARM enjoyed periods of astounding growth followed by a collapse in their share price. At its peak Bookham Technologies was worth £54 per share: that subsequently fell to close to £10 a share. Entrepreneurship requires strong nerves.

Exit

Entrepreneurs need to know when to leave a business and pass it on to a different management team. The entrepreneur who can spot and initially exploit an opportunity is not necessarily the best person to lead a company into a more mature phase of growth. Often investors and venture capitalists play a critical role at this stage of the entrepreneurial process, when the founder entrepreneur's involvement can be detrimental to business development.

Exit matters in another sense. An entrepreneurial company has to provide investors with an exit strategy to allow them to make a return on their investment. Either the company has to be sold or it has to be floated on the stock market. The prospect of being able to exit provides investors with an incentive to invest.

Conclusions

Successful entrepreneurial ventures are driven by ambitious, individual entrepreneurs who are confident, visionary, committed and determined.

But individual entrepreneurs alone do not make a business. Indeed, often they hinder a business's development if they hang on to the reins for too long. The idea of the lone hero, the maverick entrepreneur is a myth. A knowledge-based business will grow only by pulling together different talents and skills at each of the stages outlined above.

This six stage analysis of the entrepreneurial process should also make is clearer how policy can promote knowledge entrepreneurship. Intelligent policy making can make each stage of the entrepreneurial process easier by: opening up markets to create opportunities for entrepreneurs to launch new products and services; investing in spreading entrepreneurial capability; making it easier for entrepreneurs to mobilise finance, people and partners; creating networks to bring together people with ideas and know-how with venture capitalists and executive talent.

One of the main conclusions of our work is that entrepreneurs thrive amid networks which can provide them with access to ideas, partners, talent, money and customers. It is to the role of networks that we now turn.

3. Entrepreneurial networks

In a world of instant global communications, and expanding world trade and global markets, why have compact regions and cities such as Silicon Valley, Cambridge, Munich and Bangalore been at the heart of innovation? Why do tightly-knit clusters matter so much in a world in which distance appears to be waning as a constraint on economic activity?

Networks and clusters that bring together companies in the same industry, often linked to a university or knowledge base, play a vital role in innovation in knowledge driven industries. This is not a new observation. The economic analysis of clusters is more than 100 years old and especially well-recognised by historians of the Industrial Revolution. Glasgow, for example, was at the forefront of trade and engineering in the Victorian era, in large part due to a cluster of know-how around steam engines and ship building which had many of the characteristics of latter-day clusters. In Medieval times guilds clustered together in particular streets and districts of cities. Jewellers are clustered in London's Hatton Garden and the meat trades in Smithfield, to attract customers to a common location. US electronics companies are busily investing in Dresden, in eastern Germany, to tap into a pool of skilled labour left behind by the collapse of the communist micro-electronics industry.

So clusters are not new. What is new is the central role they play in knowledge-driven industries. Clusters drive innovation and entrepreneurship, which in turn helps to drive growth. That is why clusters and networks matter so much in the modern economy.

Our research shows that it is the interaction of two very different types of networks that drives innovation. First, tight networks and geographic clusters, gather innovative companies together in the same area in which they might feed from the same knowledge base. These tight clusters are facilitated by proximity to share ideas, staff and a common culture.

Second, looser international innovation networks also matter, whether in science-based industries to link up researchers, or in creative industries to get access to markets. Science-based industries, for example, are driven by collaborative international research programmes. It is difficult to be at the cutting edge of scientific research without taking part in these programmes.

Most of the successful businesses we looked at were involved in both tight and loose networks. The tight local network gave them a solid base to work from; the loose international networks allowed them to internationalise their products and the search for ideas. For example, ARM is a Cambridge based company but it sells most of its products to global mobile phone manufacturers such as Nokia. Aardman is at the core of the Bristol animation cluster but it sells much of its work to US advertising agencies and film studios. Lionhead is the most successful of a clutch computer games companies based in Guildford, but it sells its products to the likes of Sony and Nintendo.

Tight networks: clusters and innovation

Innovation at the early stages of an industry's development faces a great deal of uncertainty. Companies are not sure which kind of technology might work nor what kinds of products and services consumers might eventually buy. New ideas do not come ready made. They develop over quite long periods of trial and error, experimentation and testing, to establish what kind of approach will work best. Often embryonic technologies can be improved only by bringing together different disciplines, sharing ideas and working out how competitors have managed to create a better product. In the early days of the car industry in the late nineteenth century, for example, there were more than 2,000 companies in and around Detroit making automobiles. Henry Ford was just one among many innovators. Ford emerged as the leader of the industry thanks to his revolutionary approach to design and manufacture at lower costs. But Ford's innovation built on many other innovations developed by companies in the Detroit cluster that failed.

This process of intense experimentation, collaboration and competition requires close contact and constant communication. The more uncertain the technology and the fuzzier the market opportunity, the more communication is needed. At an early stage of an industry's development ideas and technologies have not been standardised or formatted. The knowledge developed by innovators cannot be written down in manuals. It is tacit, hard to interpret and often very localised. That is why clusters are vital to the process of innovation: they enable the intense social interaction and communication between innovators, customers, suppliers and partners that feeds innovation. There is ample evidence that despite the growth of international communications and travel, these tight knit clusters have become more important to innovation.

Even in industries such as biotechnology, in which innovation often involves the transfer of knowledge from a university into a commercial setting, these transfers are more effective when the company in question is close by on a science park. Ideas and technologies transferred out of universities invariably need considerable development to turn them into products. That requires constant interchange between academics and corporate technologists. Clusters enable know-how to flow out into industry, both through mobile labour markets, in which ideas move with people changing jobs, and through a shared milieu and institutions that help to "store" the know-how.

Collaboration to share and jointly develop ideas is only one part of the innovation process. Innovation is also driven by competition. Clusters thrive on an atmosphere of intense local rivalry, through which competing companies can compare their performance and products.

Clusters and entrepreneurship

Networks also help spawn entrepreneurs by making it easier for entrepreneurial team-based businesses to bring together the ingredients they need for growth. In Silicon Valley, for example, when an entrepreneur emerges with a promising idea they are quickly linked, usually by a venture capitalist, into a supporting network of advisers, lawyers, accountants, talent and the corporate partners they need to build a growing business. It is this combination – the drive of the entrepreneurial team and the speed with which the network assembles support for the business – that often determines whether a venture will succeed.

Networks help entrepreneurs in three primary ways:

- Networks help entrepreneurs to sense opportunities. The information sharing and job-hopping that go on within clusters help to spread knowledge about customers and emerging market opportunities, and act as a shared intelligence network for companies.
- Networks can provide companies with access to the complementary assets and resources they need to build a business: people, through a shared talent pool and mobile labour market; finance, because through referrals companies can get access to leads from venture capitalists and business angels; partners and suppliers, who provide ancillary business services to the industry.
- Networks provide a shared infrastructure not just of buildings and premises, such as a science park, but also a social and intellectual infrastructure of places to meet and share ideas. Successful clusters sometimes depend on founding institutions – like a university or a large company – to act as a hub. Sometimes they depend more on a shared milieu or atmosphere that helps to draw people together: bars, restaurants, galleries.

Different types of clusters

All knowledge-based industries need clusters and networks to innovate; but they need quite different kinds of networks to suit their needs. Very different kinds of networks have emerged in science-based industries, information technology, internet services and computer games. Clusters in each of these industries take different forms depending on the way they combine a knowledge base, location, culture, finance and governance.

To illustrate this contrast, consider the differences between the science-based clusters around Cambridge and Oxford universities and the information technology cluster along the M4 corridor; the new media cluster emerging in the east of London around Hoxton and Shoreditch and the old media clusters that have sustained animation and newspapers in London.

● *New technology clusters*
The science-based cluster of new technology companies that has emerged around Cambridge in the past two decades combines several ingredients. The founding institution is the university, which provides the formal knowledge base for many of the companies around the city, such as ARM and CDT which have spun out of the university. The university attracts talent from all around the world, some of which eventually ends up working in nearby new technology companies. The recent agreements between Cambridge University, Microsoft and MIT will underpin its international reputation.

Land near the city has been made available for the construction of science and innovation parks close to the city centre. With government funding the university is creating an entrepreneurship and innovation centre to help commercialise research more effectively.

Cambridge provides the kind of housing and quality of life that seems attractive to highly-skilled well-paid scientists: semi-detached housing, with large gardens, in semi-rural settings within driving distance of work. The reliance on cars within the Cambridge cluster, a reflection of the housing pattern, has created growing congestion.

Cambridge is within easy reach of London by train and car and three international airports (Stansted, London City and London Heathrow) are reasonably close, although local businesses are lobbying for more direct flights from the US to fly to Stansted.

The cluster has managed to spawn some large companies, among them ARM, which grew out of Acorn computers. Not only has this created role models of local success, but also a stock of expertise and financial capital in growing businesses. Amadeus, the venture capital fund run by Hermann Hauser, plays a central role in many Cambridge businesses. Cambridge has a developing infrastructure of local businesses – law firms, accountants, consultants – to help growing businesses. The Cambridge Network has been created to bring together entrepreneurs, researchers and venture capitalists to stimulate deals, but also to provide a voice for the cluster over issues such as planning and development.

Cambridge is in many respects a classic, science-based cluster. The strength of the university's knowledge base alone does not explain why so many new technology companies have been created in the area.

London, for example, is home to a majority of biotechnology research in the UK. Yet London has not spawned a biotechnology cluster because it lacks many of the ingredients – science parks, affordable semi-detached housing, a scholarly atmosphere – that attract scientific entrepreneurs. The culture, quality of life and atmosphere of Cambridge is as important in attracting science entrepreneurs as the availability of offices, transport links and finance.

The science-based cluster around Cambridge is different in many respects from the information technology corridor along the M4 and M3 motorways, stretching from Slough through Reading and Basingstoke, to Swindon and Bath. If the university is the founding institution of the Cambridge cluster, multinational information technology companies such as Cisco, Microsoft, Oracle and IBM are the founding fathers of the Thames Valley cluster. This is very much a corporate cluster rather than a university cluster. These multinational companies are attracted by a pool of skilled, mobile labour; easy access to Heathrow airport; ease of access to London, where many European company headquarters are located, and to large back-offices for banks, building societies and service companies in towns such as Basingstoke. While the Thames Valley cluster has promoted innovation, it is far less radical and more applied than the innovations emerging from Cambridge. The knowledge base in the Thames Valley is far more corporate and industrial than scientific and academic.

● *Media clusters*
Like New York, London is a media city in many respects. It is home to much of the UK's broadcasting and advertising industries. Perhaps the most famous media cluster was the concentration of national newspapers around Fleet Street, a relatively narrow and historic London street, that at one time hosted a string of print plants with newspaper offices above them. This concentration of newspapers grew up to exploit shared information and gossip on which newspapers thrived. It was held together also by the power of print trade unions which stopped newspaper publishers exploiting new technology.

However that cluster started to unravel in the early 1980s when News International moved its titles from Fleet Street to Wapping in the east end, dismissed many printers and introduced new technology. After a bitter dispute almost all other newspapers followed suit. The Mirror Group moved its editorial offices from Holborn to Canary Wharf, also the new home of the Daily Telegraph; the Express and The Star moved to Blackfriars; the Independent from City Road to Docklands; the Financial Times from St Pauls to Southwark; the Daily Mail from Fleet Street to Kensington. The reorganisation of printing was even more dramatic: many titles divested of their print plants altogether and arranged for their papers to be printed on contract in remote plants.

As this old media cluster, based on old technology and trade union power, was being dismantled and dispersed, a new media cluster was taking shape in the East End based on new technology and working practices.

Curtain Road, in Hoxton, east London, has a long a history of cultural entrepreneurship. It was the site of one of the world's first modern, Elizabethan theatres – it draws its name from the curtain that fell on the stage – as playwrights and impresarios created a new way to communicate to large audiences. These days Hoxton's run-down warehouses are home to one of the largest concentrations of new media, digital design and internet businesses in Europe.

The ingredients that have created the Hoxton cluster are completely different from the ingredients in Cambridge or along the Thames Valley corridor. It was not planned or designed by a government agency. The area benefited from subsidies provided by the European Union due to the high levels of poverty. However there never was, and still is, no plan to create a new media cluster in east London. Had there been such a plan it may well have turned people off.

There is no formal local knowledge base for the new media companies in the area. Westminster University played a covert role in supporting the area because it owns several student residential blocks in Hoxton. However none of the nearby universities, such as the Guildhall University or the University of East London played any role in providing research or a supply of talent.

There are no big media and advertising companies nearby to provide demand. The Hoxton cluster has benefited from the proximity of key London-based customers, among them banks and financial service companies, which provided early demand for web design and internet services. However no large companies have a base in the area. Indeed young new media companies located in Hoxton precisely because the traditional home for London media, Soho, is so over-priced and congested.

Venture capitalists have played only a marginal role in the growth of the Hoxton cluster. As with Silicon Alley in New York, the venture capitalists arrived only after the cluster got going: they did not kick-start it. Hoxton's new media companies have not formed a formal association akin to the Digital Media Association of New York, the non-profit organisation that was one of the founding institutions of Silicon Alley.

So how did Hoxton come to acquire a growing cluster without any of the classic ingredients which are thought to be required?

The Hoxton cluster was no accident but nor was its growth uncoordinated or unplanned. The turning point was a powerful combination of art and the internet. The large light warehouses around Curtain Road became the favoured workspaces for a new generation of young British artists, lured by cheap rents and Hoxton's reputation for being unfashionable. Gilbert and George, for many the doyennes of Britart, live and work in a Hugenot house just off nearby Brick Lane, a traditional immigrant district and home to a large Bangladeshi community. Artists such as Tracey Ermin and Damian Hirst had studios in the area and displayed their work there. Much of the work of this new generation was displayed at the Whitechapel Art Gallery which in the 1980s was directed by Nicholas Serota, who went on to become director of The Tate. Charles Saatichi, Britain's leading modern art collector, announced plans in May 2001 to open a gallery in the area. The borough of Hackney (of which Hoxton is a part) has the largest population of artists per head of population in Britain.

The development of Britart coincided with the emergence of the internet as a potential mass medium in the second half of the 1990s. Hoxton was a natural place for young internet companies to look for space, especially as some of them were founded by graduates from art and design colleges. Deepend, one of the first companies to come to Hoxton, has become one of the largest independent web design companies in London with offices in Rome, Syndey, New York and Toronto. It was founded by graduates from the Royal College of Art.

The area has become home to some of the most fashionable web design companies in London: Digit, Lateral, Tomato. And clustered around them came design companies such as Flux, software start-ups such as Anvil and communications companies. All these companies live and work cheek by jowl in the back streets of an area which has something of the feel of New York's Tribeca, an old industrial district, with large warehouses and markets, close to a major financial district.

As these developments were taking place in Hoxton, less than a mile away to the south-east Vibe Productions, a pop promotions company had become the managing agents of the eleven acre site that was the old Truman's Brewery on Brick Lane. The Brewery, surrounded by cheap curry houses, had passed through the hands of two property developers before one approached Vibe with the proposal to manage the site. Small companies – mainly music, fashion and design – started to inhabit the old office floors of the brewery. When the internet took off, the brewery became a natural home for a wave of dot.com companies. By the summer of the year 2000 there were 300 companies on the site, many of them in e-commerce. In the autumn of 2000, Gorilla Park, one of the biggest business incubators in Europe, opened a 30,000 sq foot facility just off Brick Lane, within a stone's throw of the Truman Brewery. Meanwhile more new media and design companies, among them IDEO and Moreover, were developing their base in Clerkenwell a mile west of Hoxton. This Clerkenwell–Hoxton–Brick Lane triangle is the home of London's most dynamic and thriving new media and internet cluster: it is the Silicon Alley of London.

As this agglomeration of small internet-related companies took off, so did demand for ancilliary services. Hoxton has become one of the liveliest areas in London, with a string of new bars, restaurants, clubs, cafes and sandwich shops. The close connections between fashion, art and the internet are in evidence on Hoxton Square, home to the new Lux art cinema, and London's trendiest art gallery White Cube[2]. Hoxton used to be a place people drove through on their way out of the city; now it is a place many people drive to for a night out.

Why did this network of small companies and related activities emerge in this unfashionable and overlooked triangle of east London? The main attraction of Hoxton was cheap space in warehouses of the kind that young entrepreneurs, some of them from art and design schools, wanted to work in. The established centres, like Soho, populated by large media companies, were far too expensive. These young media entrepreneurs liked Hoxton for being unfashionable because it underscored their sense that they were not part of the mainstream media world. They wanted to identify with their peers in fashion, music and art who in the mid-1990s helped to create a sense of excitement about Britain's cultural industries. There is no founding institution but art, artists, galleries and studios played a critical role in giving the area an air of creativity and cultural innovation.

When clusters succeed and fail

To succeed a cluster needs momentum and mass to get going. But as it develops it also needs a diversity of ideas and people to provide new sources of growth.

Initially a cluster is likely to grow faster around a clear base of knowledge and a distinct market opportunity. Silicon Valley, for example, got its name from companies working in the computer hardware industry, particularly in semi-conductors and disk drives. This focus helped the cluster to grow rapidly, allowing companies to share knowledge and build up expertise in a common field. Critical mass matters to any cluster: if too few companies are involved the cluster will not take off because it will not generate the level of interaction and creativity required.

Clusters focused on a single technology, market or product may grow rapidly at the outset but in the long run the very focus of these clusters is likely to become a source of vulnerability. A cluster can become congested, the victim of its own success, as property prices and wages are driven up by rapid influx of companies. A cluster can become inward looking if companies within it trade with one another too much and do not look outside for new ideas. This is the fate that befell textile machinery in Lancashire and steam engines and shipbuilding in Glasgow. A cluster with a base in a single industry or branch of technology is vulnerable to shifts in demand that leave its main product outmoded.

Any cluster is likely to face a decline in demand or rising competition in one of its industries. The key is how clusters respond. Successful clusters respond to competition with a further round of innovation to create new sources of competitive advantage. Successful clusters breed successor industries from within, based on a new generation of entrepreneurs, talent and know-how. To achieve this, clusters need to reinvest in their knowledge base often by bringing in new ideas from outside. Successful clusters have to encourage new waves of entrepreneurship. New entrants can breathe life into established clusters by challenging incumbents and opening up new pathways for local companies to grow. Silicon Valley has pulled off this trick, moving from hardware to software and services.

Loose international networks

Successful knowledge-based businesses invariably have their feet firmly rooted in a local cluster that provides them with access to their knowledge base. However, just as important, entrepreneurial knowledge-based businesses are usually highly international in their outlook from a very early stage. There is no single route to internationalisation. Animation companies, for example, are largely sustained by a domestic broadcasting and advertising market. Though international projects are common in animation they are mainly seen as akin to "exports". Computer games software, on the other hand, are an international business from the outset: the platforms and consoles are made by companies in Japan and the US; the main games publishers are based in France and the US. A British games company cannot succeed without having an international outlook from day one. The same goes for many science-based industries such as biotechnology and communications. Successful knowledge-based businesses often have to combine strong local roots, which can make them introspective, with an avowedly international outlook and a determination to match the best competitors around the world.

Access to international networks through good communications but also easy international travel matter to knowledge-based business for several reasons:

People. "Biotechnology is a global business even at the start-up stage", commented a venture capitalist, in part because there is a global labour market for research and managerial talent. Even a small industry such as animation, for example, thrives on a network of international festivals, screenings and joint-venture projects.

Research and ideas. In industries such as pharmaceuticals research is invariably conducted across collaborative international networks. Successful companies must have access to these networks to stay at the leading edge of their field. In creative industries such as web design, companies such as Digit compare themselves to and learn from companies based in the US and Japan.

Customers. Small innovative companies often attract international customers. In computer games for example, Jez San at Argonaut got his big break when Nintendo flew him to Japan to sign a deal to develop games. At ARM, Robin Saxby told his team of twelve engineers at the outset that their only hope was to think of themselves as a global company from day one, dealing with global customers such as Nokia, Ericsson and Motorola.

Partners. Often the complementary resources and expertise that companies need to develop their products are to be found elsewhere. PowderJect, for example, drew in manufacturing expertise in the US. CDT is developing polymer screens through an alliance with Epson of Japan. Oxford Asymmetry now finds itself part of a larger German biotech group.

Investors. To be credible entrepreneurial high-tech businesses have to draw on overseas investors, particularly from the US. Moreover, the internet business intelligence service, splits its operations equally between San Francisco and London. It has mainly US investors to give it credibility with US customers. Bookham Technology and ARM are quoted on the US high-tech Nasdaq market for similar reasons.

The growth of the innovation-driven knowledge economy has enhanced the importance of both tight-knit local clusters, which depend on proximity and the role of looser international networks, which are increasingly coordinated by rapid communications and efficient international travel. Successful knowledge-based businesses are invariably both firmly rooted in a local cluster and part of a wider international network, which provide them with access to different kinds of ideas, customers, partners and know-how.

In the next two chapters we examine how new industries emerge from this interaction of networks and entrepreneurship by examining the cases of computer games and animation.

4. Entrepreneurs and networks in action: computer games

Background

Britain has a world-leading position in one of the fastest growing new media sectors in the world – computer games – largely thanks to a group of young seat-of-the-pants entrepreneurs who emerged in the last decade.

This group of entrepreneurs – some of whom are profiled in this report – saw the opportunity emerging in the games industry and then developed the know-how and built the organisations to take that opportunity. Britain's strength in one of the world's fastest growing industries has little or nothing to do with government policy, venture capitalists, a formal university knowledge base nor large domestic businesses. It has been created entirely by young knowledge entrepreneurs.

By the late 1990s more than 150 British companies were developing software for computer games, according to official figures. Britain accounts for 71 per cent of the European investment in the production of computer and video games. British-developed games account for about 12 per cent of the US market and 25 per cent in Europe. The UK ranks second only to Japan in authoring computer games software. A single creation of the UK industry – Lara Croft, the heroine of Tomb Raider – earned more in overseas earnings for the UK than the Spice Girls, who in turn earned more in their peak year than some manufacturing industries.

The UK market for computer games is worth about £1 billion. That compares with £650 million spent last year in British cinemas. The world market into which British games sell, via platforms such as Sony's Playstation 2, is worth more than £12 billion or more.

Figure 1.

Platform	Global Installed base (end 1999)	Launch Date (Japan)	Sales Peak (Anticipated)
Sony Playstation	70 million	1994	1998/9
N64	22 million	1996	1999
Sega Dreamcast	2.7 million	1998	2000/1
Playstation 2	n/a	2000	n/a
Microsoft XBOX	n/a	2000	n/a
Nintendo Dolphin	n/a	2001	n/a

Source: Durlacher Research

The games industry has been promoted by waves of new technologies. Games started with very basic computers such as the Spectrum and the Commodore. They developed on more powerful personal computers and are now largely played on sophisticated games consoles that also provide access to the internet via the television. Games downloaded through a set-top box are one of the most popular features of digital television. A combination of digital television and high-bandwidth communications will allow more people to play more sophisticated games against one another online. Games will also be delivered to new generations of high-bandwidth mobile telephone services to be launched in the next few years. In a report issued in May 2001, the information consultancy Datamonitor predicted that the number of people in Europe and the US playing games online and through digital television would rise from 13 million in 2001 to more than 111 million in 2005, with revenues from that branch of the industry rising from $174 million to $5.6 billion. The opportunity for games developers who can adapt to these emerging technologies is huge.

Britain has developed a world-leading position in one of the fastest growing new media industries in the world without any of the apparent pre-requisites for growth in knowledge-based industries being present. Yet, despite, or perhaps because of that, Britain has developed a world-class industry, at least in this stage of the industry's development.

The British industry has become a success because youngsters developed the knowledge they needed to programme games by using crude early computers, such as the Spectrum and Commodre. Gaming became a community in which ideas and tips were rapidly shared, spreading knowledge. Games magazines helped to create that community, as did coding competitions, which helped to develop their skills. Many of the most successful British gamers subscribed to *Computer Video and Games*, a magazine which printed pages of code that readers could type into their machines. This was a great device for people to teach themselves to programme: if something went wrong the natural inclination was to try and fix it. Games developed a do-it-yourself culture which provided the seed bed for full-blown entrepreneurship.

The computer games industry has a distinctive knowledge base but it is largely informal and tacit. It is held in the heads and hands of largely self-taught young people. The people who write games are also their most avid consumers. Computer games developers are part of an introverted and geeky, yet creative, community, which combines collaboration and competition, creativity and technical expertise.

Several things stand out about the mainly young entrepreneurs, profiled below, who have propelled Britain into world leadership in this radiply growing industry:

- These entrepreneurs were mainly young, often fresh out of university, in the case of Peter Molyneux of Bullfrog and Lionhead Studios and Chris van der Kuyl of VIS Interactive. Jez San at Argonaut wrote his first game while still at school. They rarely had conventional careers.
- Their motivation for going into business was partly negative, to avoid working for a large corporation and partly a desire to do something creative with computers. Although many wanted to "have a hit" few went into business as a way to make money.
- The computer games industry has been driven by a do-it-yourself culture, which has built up a strong shared but informal knowledge base. Access to this community was vital to successful entrepreneurship in the industry. Ian Stewart, who is not a games developer and is a generation older than most of the other entrepreneurs in the industry, got access to the community through his Sheffield

software shop. Lesley Keen, of Inner Workings, one of the few women in the industry, in part failed because she felt so at odds with the adolescent male culture which still dominates the industry.

- All the entrepreneurs sensed the emerging opportunity of computer games thanks to their distinctive knowledge, which in turn came from being close to innovative consumers. They had the self-confidence to articulate that opportunity to other people. Jez San did this by showing Nintendo executives a demo of a 3-D game for its Gameboy hand-held console. Ian Stewart sensed where the market was heading by understanding how kids used computers in his shop.

- Opportunity is being created in the games industry by waves of new technology for authoring games and new platforms to play them on. Sensing opportunity is not a one-off event, but a continual process in an industry driven by change. As a result timing is vital: Lesley Keen's company Inner Workings failed in part because it jumped on the wrong technological boat: multimedia edutainment for CD-roms.

- The entrepreneurs were confident and visionary but also deeply opportunistic and pragmatic. Capitalising on chance played a critical role in several of their stories.

- They were all adept at adapting to change. Chris van der Kuyl has a long-term vision for his company VIS Interactive but admits that he can plan at most two years ahead. Having invested in multimedia van der Kuyl had to buy back his company from investors to take it into games. Ian Stewart went through a similar upheaval at Gremlin.

- Most leapt from self-financing their business to drawing in venture capital or even taking their company private. As a result many missed out intermediate stages of funding – largely because such finance is so hard to raise – that could have built the business over a longer period. In the case of Gremlin and Inner Workings, the lack of this intermediate finance meant they were under-capitalised and had to grow too fast from too small a base.

- The successful entrepreneurs recognised that they had to build a team of people around them with complementary skills. The businesses that were run as a one-man show generally failed.

Figure 2. History of games hardware

1976 –80	The first consoles, led by the Atari VCS 2600, create a market for games.
1980 – 1989	The age of programmable home computers, particularly important in the UK. Machines include Spectrum, Acorns, Commodores etc.
1989 – 1993	The market consolidates around two consoles from Sega and Nintendo. PCs begin to make inroads into the home.
1994-5	The market for consoles remains flat or declines as a new generation of machines are anticipated from Sega, Nintendo and new entrant – Sony.
1996 – present	Three new products – the Sony Playstation, Nintendo 64 and the Sega Saturn – cause market to expand. More than 5 million UK households now have a PC, across Europe as a whole, PC is the dominant games platform.
1999 – 2002	Release of a revised version of the Sony Playstation and the Sega Dreamcast. Concern that "platform wars" could stifle development in some quarters. It addition to the "big three" of Sega, Sony and Nintendo, Microsoft plans to enter the fray with its console code-named X Box. This makes it likely that no one box will dominate the market as the Sony Playstation did in the late 1990s and will increase development costs significantly.

Jez San, Argonaut Software, London

Jez San, in common with other computer games entrepreneurs, got into computers early. His father worked in import-export, and bought him a home computer in the US before they were available here. He was twelve years old.

"I found something I wanted to do, I was the nerdy teenage computer-hacker type". He became a "gamer", and although he passed the requisite number of O levels, by the time it got to A levels, he was more interested in, "computers, programming and staying up late to play games."

" So I didn't go to university, which was probably the best thing for me," he says, "although later in life, I thought it might have been fun. But then I probably wouldn't have had the same opportunities."

To a young man, with surplus creative energy, the nascent games industry was a godsend. His first game, Skyline Attack, didn't make any money. His second, Starglider took "two years of my life at home in my bedroom." Starglider sold several hundred thousand copies, of which San made about £2 a copy. "Which for a guy with no expenses, in his bedroom, was ... plenty of money."

With the proceeds he got himself an office and hired some other employees. They did a lot of R & D: "We tried to do things that were 'cooler' than everyone else technically, even if perhaps not creatively at the time."

This investment in knowledge creation led to a breakthrough in the early 1990s. The Nintendo Gameboy console was already a success when San and his colleagues reverse engineered it to play a 3-D game. San approached someone from Nintendo at a trade show: "I thrust the Gameboy in his face and said, 'look what we can do'. It was something they'd never seen before: 3-D graphics on a Gameboy. No one dreamed it was possible."

Nintendo flew San to Japan and hired his company, Argonaut to develop three games in a multi-million dollar deal. Only two games were released, but one of them, Starfox, sold 4 million copies to become one of the best-selling games ever. It made Argonaut "a fortune" according to San. The company grew from fifteen to 100 people.

During the collaboration with Nintendo, San and others from Argonaut suggested to Nintendo that they design some hardware that would improve their machine. Nintendo took a gamble and financed a joint-venture company – which resulted in the Super FX chip, the basis for 3-D games machines. More than 10 million chips have been sold. Argonaut subsequently spun out its hardware arm into a separate company, ARC, which along with Argonaut subsequently floated on the stock market.

Argonaut started by only making games for Nintendo, "which made us a bit under their thumb". The end of the exclusive relationship with Nintendo and the need to develop games for all platforms meant that, in 1997, Argonaut ceased to rely just on its own funds for organic growth and instead it sought venture capital to develop the business.

The investors included Japanese publishers, Koei, New Media Investors and Apax Partners in London. In March 2000 Argonaut raised £18 million in a flotation. Its revenues in the year to October 2000 were £4.4 million and it made a pre-tax loss of £636,000. San remarked: "Having demanding financial institutions is good. It made us more mature. They demanded reports, they demanded board meetings – all that stuff made us grow up."

Argonaut's strategy to develop games for many platforms has born fruit. The first "Croc" game sold more than 1 million copies and its successor Croc2 was also a success. Income from royalties was up 60 per cent to £1.6 million in 2000 while income from advances for future games was £28 million. Argonaut's financial position had strengthened its hand with publishers: "Being well-financed helps a great deal. Normally games developers will go to a publisher with a prototype or concept, so the publisher is taking a big risk at that point, so the deal isn't going to be very good. But if you can afford to develop more of the game and show them something that is nearly finished, you'll get a much better deal."

San recognised early on that Argonaut, "was a beast that needed taming", and that he couldn't run the whole thing himself. However, he argues that the inherent creativity and unpredictability of games development means it is not amenable to standard management techniques: "All you can predict about games its that they will be late. This makes planning quite hard and you have to operate a portfolio approach. Unlike other software, its always cutting edge, its always R&D – it's not structured. If you're selling an accounts package, you want it to do what every accounts package has done before – your feature is 100 per cent compatibility – our feature is to do what's no one's expected or has seen before."

Peter Molyneux, Lionhead Studios, Guildford, Surrey

Lionhead Studios, one of the best-known games developers in the UK, occupies unremarkable offices in the Surrey Business Park near Guildford. The door handles give the game away: they are in the shape of a Pac Man. Peter Molyneux, the founder and managing director, shares an open plan office with other developers. The atmosphere is informal and family-like. In one corner young boys test games for free. Kids have come from as far afield as Germany to test Molyneux's games.

Molyneux always wanted to have his own business. Even as a child, he "had a passion for it." He formed his first business at school: arranging for other kids to cut people's lawns. From an early age Molyneux was a game player: computers changed his life.

Molyneux is dyslexic. He found school difficult and was regarded as stupid. "I can remember being very frustrated as a child not having any creative outlets. Suddenly these things called computers came along and it was like this God-given machine for my skills."

His first job brought him into contact with an entrepreneur and role model, Sean Posten, who built the country's biggest mail-order sports equipment business. Molyneux, fresh from university was sent to work for Posten by the local dole office, to reprogramme the company's tele-sales systems. "The experience of watching this bloke with his enthu-siasm and being trusted to set all these things up was incredible. I've used that experience time and time again."

Through contacts he had made working with Posten, Molyneux got together with a friend, Les Edgar, to set up Taurus Acquisition to make database software. The company was funded by credit cards.

There is more than an element of luck in the Peter Molyneux story. "One day, out of the blue, we were rung up by Commodore – this global electronics company – who said 'We'd really like your product on our machine, can you come and see us about how we can do that?'" Molyneux and Edgar went along. Commodore was preparing to launch the powerful Amiga. As the meeting ended Commodore agreed to send five top-range Amigas to Molyneux's office. It was at that point that it dawned on him that Commodore had called up the wrong Taurus. "They had phoned us instead of 'Torus,' a company that did network cards."

Molyneux and Edgar kept silent and got their five machines When eventually they showed Commodore a demonstration of the game they had developed Commodore executives were still keen. Through this fortuitous step Molyneux moved into the games industry.

Bullfrog
Edgar and Molyneux founded Bullfrog Productions Ltd to develop games. The first – Populous – went on to sell 4 million copies. Populous was a new type of computer game – a strategy game in which the player takes the role of a deity ruling over minions. This kind of game later became known generically as a 'god-sim' game and spawned hundreds of imitators. Populous is one of the ten most successful computer games of all time.

"Life gets a lot easier when you've had a big hit. I wasn't some great guru sitting there thinking, 'what's gonna sell three and a half million copies?' I was some pizza-eating, coke guzzling geek who said, um, let's do a game about this. That was as much insight as I had into it."

Molyneux explains his success by the blend of skills he brings to games. He says he is a competent programmer and though he is an atrocious artist he can visualise what a game should look like. Molyneux believes his main skill is being able to convey things very clearly to people. "Sitting down with someone and saying, this is how the game should be, this is how we should approach it. It's the clarity of the vision that I give to people. It's more of a directorial skill."

"After the success of Populous we could have taken that money and cashed in there, but instead we really felt there was going to be a future in computer games." Molyneux went onto do three other games for Bullfrog – Powermonger, Populous 2 and Syndicate. Even at this stage in the early 1990s, with a major hit under their belts, Bullfrog only employed about ten people. By the time Magic Carpet was released in 1994, the company employed about 30 people. It had produced five consecutive number-one hits, a record unique in the industry and was starting to attract offers to buy the business from large companies, which the founders turned down. When Theme Park, which allows players to plan and develop their own theme park, was released and sold more than 3 million copies, Bullfrog's valuation shot through the roof.

Molyneux and Edgar sold their company for $40 million of shares in Electronic Arts, the US publisher. By the time the deal was completed and Edgar and Molyneux had cashed in their chips they were worth $60 million.

"Financially, it was wonderful. I had a ton of money in the bank. I was having lunches at Goldman Sachs. It was a very big social change for both Les and me. We both bought fast cars and we both bought big houses. However Bullfrog had always been my emotional crutch. EA wanted to expand Bullfrog hugely. Over eighteen months Bullfrog went from 35-40 people to just under 100. I went from somebody who did most of the design on the games and an awful lot of the programming to someone who was managing a hundred people."

He admits that for a time he had "stupidly thought" that he wanted to change EA itself, the largest games publisher in the world. Molyneux quickly realised he wasn't cut out to be a corporate executive: "There were an awful lot of board meetings. It is incredibly boring, very, very tedious and didn't suit my personality at all."

Molyneux also knew he could not spend the rest of his life running Bullfrog: he no longer enjoyed running the company. So Molyneux decided to make his exit and leave.

Lionhead Studios

It seemed obvious to Molyneux that his next move would be to start another company. "Even having an extended weekend is like death to me. I start panicking and thinking 'what am I going to do?' If I'm not part of that process of creation, I feel terrible." Computer games have been Molyneux's way to defuse that panic.

The idea behind Lionhead was to re-create Bullfrog when it was a highly creative, twenty person company. "It was so much fun then and the people there were so creative, it was just a wonderful period of my life. In terms of creativity and the atmosphere Lionhead has surpassed anything that Bullfrog was before by a factor of ten."

Molyneux's first game with Lionhead is Black & White, which aims to take game playing onto another level of interactive sophistication. Most computer games are still emotionally primitive, based on skills of speed and tactics. Film and television drama on the other hand can be emotionally engaging while not allowing for much interaction. "Games have the capacity to allow you to supply emotions to characters in a very real way, in a way a movie will never be able to do. You will be able to interact with a piece of entertainment and, as a result of your interaction, that piece of entertainment changes. There are some technical mountains to climb before we can say, we have characters in our games who can display emotions and react to your emotions. But we'll get there." Black & White was released in 2001.

Lesley Keen, Inner Workings, Glasgow

Lesley Keen was an unusual person to be running a company that developed computer games. Not only is a she a woman, rare enough in this industry, but she came to games late after a career spanning several aspects of what she terms, "interactive home entertainment."

When we first interviewed Keen in autumn 1998, she was running Inner Workings – a Glasgow-based company employing some 70-odd staff, specialising in children's games. It had been trading since the early 1990s. In summer 1999 the company was wound up. Keen's story exemplifies the fragility of the UK computer games market.

Background
Keen's background was in animation, but unlike most traditional animators she has been involved with computer graphics since the mid-1970s. At a multimedia show in Olympia in London she met someone demonstrating an interactive CD. A consortium of people, including Phillips, approached her to do a project about Ancient Egypt.

Keen took the opportunity to get into interactive media and founded Inner Workings. "At the beginning it was me and a couple of colleagues in my attic, with a small amount of seed capital from Scottish Enterprise (£25,000 to buy machines), working on the first project for Philips. That was 1992."

The product never came to market because Inner Workings, which was doing the graphics, could not work with the programmers who were part of the Philips consortium. Keen believed that Inner Workings needed to combine all the creative disciplines – programming, sound and graphics – under one roof. "We couldn't see how our creative vision could materialise unless we were controlling it."

The next venture was a four-title commission to make CD-roms for Oxford University Press (OUP), as a result of which OUP made a small investment in Inner Workings. The idea was to help OUP move into multimedia by putting some of its children's books on to CD. By 1995, the market for "edutainment" was looking quite exciting. But suddenly at the start of 1996 it went pear-shaped: the hype about creating multimedia versions of books burst.

It was a theme that would reoccur in Inner Workings' life: the company had backed the wrong technology and needed to change tack quickly. Inner Workings had already gone public on AIM, London's financial market for small and growing companies. Having benefited only partially from the original multimedia 'hype' that had gripped the City, Inner Workings nevertheless got caught in the backlash against multimedia that rapidly followed it.

By 1996, Keen knew that the company had to start making original material rather than repurposing existing material. She took Inner Workings into games. Although she felt she had the money to finance the transition, the real difficulty was the "quite different life forms you meet in the games industry."

The shift came too late for Inner Workings, which also missed out on the surge of internet stocks in the late 1990s. "We ran out of money" is all that Keen will say in elaboration of what happened to Inner Workings.

A variety of factors played a role in Inner Workings demise. The company suffered from mis-timing. It sensed an opportunity for games but it was too early and too poor to take it: "What we predicted would happen to the Playstation and what we were basing our strategy on, that is, that the price would drop drastically making it viable for children, has happened. But it has happened too late for us."

Keen found it difficult to assemble the managerial support she needed to make the company fly. The gap between innovative new companies, exploiting new technologies and potential investors also hurt. In the early days when she was pitching to investors Keen had to explain what multimedia was and why there was a future for computer games: "A lot of things I had to explain are common knowledge now, which makes me wonder, are you wise to be a pioneer?"

Inner Workings started life undercapitalised and in many ways, remained so despite its listing on AIM. "We went to the market too early, seduced by the notion that we could bypass the venture capital loop and keep hold of equity." At the end, she says Inner Workings would have needed 18 months or two years to turn the company around: "But we couldn't get the lifeline."

By the time Inner Workings' shares were suspended it had six games titles in development, about 60 programme developers, it was spending close to £1 million a year on games development and yet it had little it could show the City, at least in terms of publishing contracts for the games.

When asked whether she wanted to become an entrepreneur, Keen, unlike most of the entrepreneurs interviewed in this project, replied: "Absolutely not." She originally thought of herself as an artist and animator, and resistant to being involved in commerce. "I find business fascinating but I also want a life."

Keen was unusual: a woman in an industry closely identified with adolescent boys, of all ages. She reflected: "I was not discriminated against but as a life-form I was completely different. I discovered that this business was a kind of religion. It's like Hollywood, people want to be part of the buzz, but when you are part of it, it's hideous."

Chris van der Kuyl, VIS Interactive, Dunfermline

Chris van der Kuyl has been involved in the computer industry for as long as he can remember. Before going to university, he worked in games shops, which gave him the idea of running his own business. This ambition was confirmed when, while studying computer science at university, he did a placement with computer company NCR in the US. His experience of working for a high tech multinational convinced him: "There was no way on this planet I wanted to go and work for one of those companies."

After leaving university and training in digital video techniques, van der Kuyl got his first contract and started VIS with an overdraft and a small loan from the Prince's Youth Business Trust. One of his main motivations was to stay in Scotland: he did not become an entrepreneur to make money.

Van der Kuyl desperately wanted to expand the business and found an investor in the shape of a local PR and marketing company that was looking to expand into multimedia. They offered to buy VIS and in exchange van der Kuyl took a 25 per cent stake in the new combined company.

After another year, at the end of 1994, it became clear the multimedia market was not growing in the way they had hoped. The games market, however, was coming out of a downturn. However, to shift VIS into games required serious investment. Van der Kuyl asked his backers for £1 million: "They promptly told us to get stuffed."

At this point, van der Kuyl engineered a management buyout and set about recruiting some professional management. For him, the critical rule as an entrepreneur is : "To know that you could do it yourself – but to get somebody else in who can do it better."

The chief executive of the communications group that had previously owned VIS left his company to join van der Kuyl. He also brought in Ian Ritchie, President of the British Computer Society and a successful entrepreneur in his own right. Ritchie invested in VIS and became chairman (a position he has since left). Following Ian Ritchie's departure van der Kuyl hired Les Edgar, co-founder with Peter Molyneux of Bullfrog in Guildford.

The three founders of the next stage of the company's growth invested enough of their own money to keep VIS going for about nine months. They signed their first game, Headz, to Hasbro, and within a few months they got their first venture capital investment, £1 million from 3i, Scottish Development Finance (part of Scottish Enterprise) and a syndicate of private investors. Since then VIS has signed several more projects, including a joint-venture with Flextech-Telewest to create content for interactive digital television, shipped several games and closed the second round of venture capital funding at three times the valuation of the first round.

Van der Kuyl has his critics in the Scottish games industry. Yet he is acknowledged by most commentators to have great publicity skills that have stood him in good stead when it comes to raising funds. After a third round of funding VIS employs about 100 staff and operates several studios.

Ian Stewart, ex-Gremlin Group, Sheffield

Ian Stewart was involved in the games industry from its very inception. However Stewart has never developed a game. His skills are in management and retailing. Stewart helped to build Gremlin, in its time one of the most successful computer games companies in the UK. After its sale to French group Infogrammes, Stewart became a venture capitalist with NM Rothschild.

Stewart began his career working for Lasky's, the hi-fi and computer shop as a retail manager. This gave him first hand insight into the beginnings of the home computer boom. Stewart sensed there was an emerging opportunity to sell software and support along with hardware to the domestic market.

Stewart grew frustrated with Lasky's and decided to go into business himself. Stewart sold his house to open a games software shop. It was the first shop of its kind in Sheffield and one of only a few in the country.

At that time in the early 1980s most computer games came from the US. A few came from pioneer developers in the UK, such as Ocean in Liverpool. As Stewart was looking for games to sell, he started to examine some of the UK games development companies to see what they were doing. "And I thought, I could do that."

A clique of boys used to come into Stewart's shop, often bearing demos of games they had made. Stewart identified a couple with above average ability and employed them in the office above the shop to design games. This was in 1983. In those days you could design a game with three or four people.

Having set up a small development studio, he realised he knew nothing about distribution. Stewart formed a publishing and distribution company with his partner from the shop, a programmer to develop the games and someone from a distribution company that advised him. Thus Gremlin was born.

Gremlin grew quickly. In those it took only six months to develop a game. As the portfolio grew, more staff were recruited. However the programmer partner to the venture decided he no longer wished to be involved. The other partners agreed to buy out his 25 per cent share, but as Stewart explained: "The guy from the distribution company, was the one with the money. Everything we earned had gone back into the business." Stewart and his partner found their stakes heavily diluted. They ended up with 11 per cent from their original 25 per cent stake.

Nevertheless the business continued to do well. The distribution arm grew into one of the largest in the UK. But Stewart felt the games development part of the company was not getting enough attention. In 1989, Stewart put together a management buy-out with his wife, Jenny. He funded it by yet again mortgaging his house.

Stewart acknowledges this was high risk. But he and his wife knew the business. "The thing is, when you have opportunities like that, you have to be confident in your own abilities." Stewart restructured the company and brought in two senior executives, one in charge of development and the other in operations. The new Gremlin started its new life with 21 people.

The most important thing in business, he says, is to get the right advice at the right time. "A lot of people think they can make do with cheap advice, but it's a false economy." He took advantage of a DTI scheme, which gave him a £10,000 contribution to have some professional consultants offer some strategic advice. "We were profitable at that stage, but needed to be more confident in knowing what to do next," explained Stewart. "The consultant's report laid the foundation for the next three or four stages of Gremlin's growth."

Gremlin grew steadily from twenty employees to about 75. The company went public on the London Stock Exchange at the end of 1997. At that time the company employed around 200 people. "Jenny and I were looking at ways of ensuring the continued growth, as well as realising some of our own wealth." At the end of 1998, Gremlin issued a profits warning, following worse than expected sales of a number of key titles. By May 1999, Gremlin's share price had collapsed. French publisher Infogrammes, eventually acquired Gremlin for £24 million.

The future of the games industry
The market for British-developed computer games is expanding, with more games being played by more people on more devices and platforms. The downside is that the home-grown DIY British industry may face more capable, better funded competitors who may be more able to make the most of new technologies. Successful games developers may well need deeper pockets to develop more complex games. An industry that has relied on self-taught programmers may require more formal training and education to develop deeper technical skills. The British cottage industry that thrived when computer games were in their infancy might find itself out gunned.

Strengths
The British computer games industry, created by this wave of entrepreneurship in the 1980s and 1990s, has several strengths.

● *Community and critical mass*
Britain has developed a critical mass of games developers, a strong community of knowledge to build upon and an educated, innovative

market of users. It is known by global games publishers as a source for first class content.

● *Role models and talent*
The industry's success is breeding role models – Molyneux, San, van der Kuyl – who have inspired others to follow in their footsteps. Computer games will be an attractive industry for people that want to work creatively with computers and not in a large organisation or e-business.

● *Scale of opportunity*
The opportunity for British computer games is expanding rapidly from computers to television and mobile telephones. The tools for creating games are getting more sophisticated. A generation that grew up with computer games is in work: they will increasingly be open to the 3-D games format as a visual gateway to the internet and other forms of entertainment and information.

● *Creativity*
British developers have a creative open style which leaves them well-placed to take these opportunities. "We're an eccentric culture of intro-verts," says Jez San "There are a lot of Brits about who are into comput-ers and programming. Its part of pop culture." John Sutherland from Abertay University, which set up the first university course for computer games developers, says the variety of UK-produced games is a source of strength. "We are eccentric, creative and less conformist than other European countries. The Japanese and Americans produce a more limited range of styles of games. Only the British like and develop all sorts of games."

Weaknesses
Yet the industry's strengths are also in many respects a source of its main weaknesses:

● *Skills and complexity*
The industry is becoming more complex. As technology for authoring and playing games becomes more sophisticated, so too do the kinds of knowledge required. The DIY culture which got the British industry off

to a flying start might hold it back in future. When computer games first emerged the industry attracted self-taught programmers. As technology and games have become more complex so the industry has started to compete for talent that could be taken into consulting, financial services or business software.

● *Development costs*
The resources needed to compete in the modern games industry are increasingly beyond the reach of the average British company. These days it takes anything up to £1 million or twenty staff years to develop a computer game. Some games take three years to develop.

● *Project management skills*
The rising complexity and expense of developing games means there will be a premium on project management skills. Nick Gibson at Durlacher says many companies lack experienced management of the kind that outside investors like to see in a company. "People invest in management This is one of the reasons why Chris van der Kuyl has been so successful at raising money for VIS. It is quite dynamically run. Investors believe he can take the company forward."

● *Publishing power*
Britain's strength in developing games belies its weakness in marketing and publishing them, where US companies such as Electronic Arts and French companies such as Infogrammes and Havas International, part of the Vivendi-Universal media group, are far stronger. Games development is a hit and miss, fashion-driven business. Publishing, marketing and distributing games is less risky. The publishers have power in the industry.

● *Cottage industry culture*
Too few of the British companies have ambitions to become solid companies. As a result the industry is unlikely to attract sustained investment. John Sutherland at Abertay University describes computer games entrepreneurs thus: "They have a garage mentality. Not enough of them want to be Microsoft. They don't know-how to scale up and there are a lot of small, vulnerable companies across the UK. All they see is the next

game. They don't live to build the business. Too much money is creamed – note the preponderance of red Ferraris in games' company car parks – there is not enough long-term planning."

In a highly volatile industry, Britain's vulnerable companies may lack the clout and scale to keep the industry at the forefront of the global market. British companies will lack not just financial resources, but also ambition and management skills to grow.

● *Geek culture*

While the potential market for games is vast, computer games are still made by geeks for geeks. Peter Molyneux explained: "The games industry will never become higher profile until it becomes mass market. It's all very well to have games that get harder and harder to play. But you just appeal to the same people that bought your games last time. The games we produce tend to be about killing, maiming, mass murdering – boys with big toys. What we don't have is many women in the industry, and it's incredibly hard to attract them in. We have to open up this industry and make it more accessible to the general public."

Prospects and policies

Five critical areas need urgent attention if the British computer games industry is to maintain its position as a world leader and spawn new generations of entrepreneurs who can grow substantial companies.

Skills

To secure the skills it needs the games industry needs to form closer links with education.

The industry is increasingly staffed by graduates. Peter Molyneux at Lionhead tends to recruit people with maths, physics or computer science skills, but also philosophy graduates who have a logical and creative mind. Molyneux argues it takes no more than three months to train them in the specific skills of games programming. In Scotland skill shortages are more pressing, complains Chris van der Kuyl, although Scotland has the largest number of computer graduates per head of population of any country in Europe, according to Scottish Enterprise.

This also changes the demands on entrepreneurs. Team building is a critical part of Molyneux's job: "You have to match people who have a huge amount of skill – and nowadays you're talking about people who have firsts from Cambridge or Edinburgh – in a way that they get on and feel totally dedicated towards producing an incredibly important game." The computer games industry is increasingly competing with "normal industries and normal careers," for programmers with extraordinary talents. "To compete in the world now you have to have hugely talented people, it's not as it was when you could teach yourself programming and come up with a game. We are talking about very bright people who are extremely expensive."

The UK's first computer games' courses were developed at Abertay University in Dundee to sustain the local industry. John Sutherland, the course tutor explained: "We have – but not by design – the world's first MSc and BSc courses in computer games writing. These were created after pressure from local games companies – DMA and VIS – and started with the MSc in 1997, followed by the BSc in 1998." Abertay also offers a Computer Arts BA, which mixes games design with music, audio and animation skills. Entry requirements, especially for maths and programming, are very high. Applications outstrip the number of places available by a factor of ten.

The Abertay course seeks to turn out designers rather than businessmen, though students can study entrepreneurship courses in their final year. In addition, most students take courses in Japanese and marketing. About 30 students a year take up placements with Japanese companies. Other universities are starting to follow Abertay's lead: Bradford, Salford, Teeside and Middlesex are offering games-related courses to undergraduates.

Sutherland designed the course in close collaboration with Dundee-based computer games companies. Local games companies contribute in kind usually through teaching. Sutherland has started working with Scottish Enterprise and the local authority to encourage games start-ups, in part through a ten-week summer school for budding entrepreneurs.

Management

As games companies take on more complex, demanding and bigger development projects, so classic project management skills will become more critical. Chris van der Kuyl acknowledged that VIS Interactive needs a core of experienced managers to supplement the young graduate developers.

Computer games companies might get people with these skills by recruiting from the mainstream IT industry. An alternative would be to make available timely packages of management courses and external management advice to companies.

Finance

Computer games companies need access to more imaginative tools for financing growth. There is a yawning gap between self-finance and sweat equity, of the kind that will develop companies of up to ten to twenty people, and venture capital that will take a company into high levels of growth and eventual flotation. One answer may be the growing use of completion bonds to raise bank finance. A developer can take a publisher's contract to publish a game and use that as security to borrow from a bank. Another might be to create special government-backed lending facilities for growth companies.

Infrastructure

Computer games producers are innovative when they are working closely with innovative, young customers. In the industry's early days those kids worked with quite primitive computers at home, bought from shops like Laskys. But in future much of the innovation will take place online as more computer games, especially multi-player games, are delivered online. A country with a poor broadband telecommunications infrastructure is unlikely to generate innovative usage among consumers and so is less likely to sustain an innovative games production industry. As Chris van der Kuyl puts it: "In the knowledge economy, the only piece of infrastructure that really matters is telecommunications. And right now it's crap because it is too expensive. The online gaming community is big and would be bigger. Unless we can sort it out, we're stuffed. From a commercial point of view, what in the US would cost me between $5K and $10K a year, I'm being quoted between £60 and £70K a year. I'm dealing with guys in LA and New York and they want me to deliver software to them, (via the net) we just can't do it 'cos the cost is so great for a company of our size. We are being absolutely stiffed. For a high tech business, it's the biggest problem."

Networks

The computer games industry started out as a self-help industry among consumers who were also games producers. An industry that started as a digital cottage industry will need to become both more professional and better organised. Successful companies, created in the first wave of the industry's growth can play a role. Peter Molyneux, together with Steve Jackson, founder of Games Workshop, who also works for Lionhead, is helping games start-ups through his "satellite scheme" he runs with US publisher Activision. Lionhead takes an equity share of less than 50 per cent in the start-up and negotiates on behalf of smaller companies with the publishers. Lionhead also gives them access to its technology, which can take months off the development time for the first game. The first two companies in the satellite scheme were Big Blue Box and Intrepid.

The most determined attempt to mobilise the games community into a network has been the Scottish Games Alliance (SGA).

Once upon a time, the Scottish games industry boiled down to one company, DMA, the creator of the hit game Lemmings, based in Dundee. It might have stayed that way had it not been for the collaboration between Scottish entrepreneurs and Scottish Enterprise the economic development agency, which spawned the Scottish Games Alliance.

A Scottish Enterprise team had been looking at the indigenous software industry since 1991, initially focusing on the strengths of the Scottish universities in artificial intelligence, robotics, financial services and super-computers. In the mid-1990s, Robin Mair began editing the *Software Echo*, a monthly journal for the industry published by Scottish Enterprise, which began to carry articles about games companies.

The reasons for the industry's strength in Scotland, Mair argues, include: the largest number of computer science graduates per capita in Europe; the broad nature of Scottish Highers – the equivalent of English A levels – which help Scottish students develop the full range of technical and business skills as well as creativity; Scottish arts schools, which have provided a lot of computer-related courses.

Mair and Chris van der Kuyl got talking about the number of computer games companies in Scotland's central belt that did not know each other. They agreed the companies would benefit from getting together, if only informally, to discuss common issues such as recruitment. The SGA grew from that seed.

The computer games industry in Scotland is relatively small, with no significant publishers and no large companies such as Eidos. However, according to Robin Mair and others, new firm formation continues to be healthy. Figure 3 shows the relative position of the SGA members in 1998/99. Two companies missing from this table, who were members of the SGA in 1998 are Lesley Keen's Inner Workings, which went into receivership and DMA, which was taken over by Gremlin and then sold to French publisher Take 2. The SGA no longer classifies DMA as a Scottish company.

Figure 3. SGA members, 1998/99

Ranking	Company	Turnover (£m)	No. of Employees
1 (7)	Red Lemon Studios	1.12 (0.53)	40 (20)
2 (3)	Visual Sciences	1.0 (1.2)	49 (33)
3 (2)	VIS Interactive	0.72 (1.24)	65*
4 (8)	Absolute Studios	0.41 (-)	14 (7)
5 (5)	I-Design	0.35 (0.34)	11 (9)
6 (6)	Steel Monkeys	-	18

Source: Scottish Games Alliance
Note: Previous year's figures are in brackets
*Now 100 after recent takeovers

The SGA was formed in December 1996. Although the Scottish games companies are fiercely competitive, they operate in a very large international market. They rarely compete with one another directly. "We are all in the same business, but we are not fighting for the same publishing deals," says DMA's Brian Baglow. There is an understanding that members of the SGA will not poach staff from one another, but there is no enforcement mechanism if the rule is violated.

The SGA was set up with six founding games development companies to improve PR, enhance the industry's credibility and aid recruitment in part by improving links with academia. The SGA runs a website (www.scottigames.org), a Scottish developers' lounge at trade shows, seminars and regular meetings for the chief executives of the main companies, as well as product competitions.

Full members pay £500 and are featured on the website. One of the SGA's biggest successes has been its presence at trade shows. E3 is a games industry trade show that takes place in the US. At a recent E3 meeting an estimated £7 million of deals were signed by Scottish companies.

The SGA is still young and relatively small. Its supporters argue that it has established enough of a critical mass to help the Scottish industry develop. One promising development for the British industry as a whole was the recent establishment of Tiga, the independent games alliance, to provide some of the same services across the UK industry as a whole.

Conclusion

The British computer games industry is at a critical point in its development. A community of largely self-taught developers has turned itself into a world class industry. The next few years will prove whether it will suffer the fate of earlier innovative British industries, built on a mixture of entrepreneurship and DIY knowledge – shipbuilding in Glasgow, textile machinery in Lancashire – which were unable to meet better organised, funded and skilled foreign competition as the market matured. The first wave of knowledge entrepreneurs in the industry have created an enormous opportunity, which policy makers, investors and educators need to play a role in helping future generations to entrepreneurs to exploit.

5. Entrepreneurs and networks in action: animation

The UK's animation industry punches well above its weight. The industry's international reputation, based on Oscar-winners such as Wallace and Gromit (made by Aardman), belies the fragility of many companies within it. Local production clusters, combined with extensive international networks, sustain the industry and protect it from the volatility of the companies that make it up.

Animation in the UK is largely a creative, craft industry, made up of small companies working on relatively low-budget projects for smaller markets. Almost two-thirds of UK animation companies employ fewer than ten animators. Only 5 per cent employ more than 25. According to one of the most comprehensive surveys of the UK animation industry (undertaken by the consultancy SCPR for Skillset, the training organisation for the film, video and TV and multimedia sectors, in June 1998) the industry employs between 3,000 and 3,500 people in about 300 animation companies in England and Wales. Almost 20 per cent of respondents had an annual gross income of under £12,000 and only a tenth earned above £40,000.

One contrast puts the UK industry's position in international perspective. The US animation industry has produced hundreds of hours of long-running animation series, such as the Simpsons, not to mention South Park and Disney's feature length cartoons. Yet there are only three and a half hours of finely crafted Wallace and Gromit animated films. As in several other industries Britain's strength lies not in volume production by large companies, but in high valued-added craft production by relatively small companies.

The industry overcomes the fragility of the firms that make it up, thanks to the local clusters and international networks that sustain it. While individual companies are often small and vulnerable, the animation sector as a whole has greater resilience and flexibility thanks to these networks. The animation industry exemplifies why a combination of local clusters and international networks matter in an industry. Small animators are sustained by working in close proximity to one another to share ideas, talent and contacts. Animation is a small industry in world terms. Quite a lot of animation projects are international joint-ventures, which require pooled funding and collaboration between teams working in different countries. The international networks that organise the industry – through animation festivals for example – are as vital as the local clusters. A small company will be extremely fragile if isolated. However as animation shows it will be strengthened if it finds itself in a strong local cluster, such as that emerging in Bristol around Aardman and with access to these international networks.

Fragility

British animation thrives on a sense of creative community. Most animators aspire not to riches but to creative success and critical acclaim. Animation entrepreneurs tend to run small businesses, with limited ambitions for growth. Most are happy simply to survive and make a living. They have neither the markets nor the capital to sustain larger companies.

British animation highlights how the scope for entrepreneurship is conditioned by many factors: it is rarely simply the product of the drive of the individual entrepreneur. British animation businesses are constrained by the opportunities available to them. They mainly work for national broadcasters or advertisers, often on relatively small budgets for children's programmes. That is one reason why animation is home to micro-entrepreneurship. Entrepreneurs with ambitions for rapid growth would not be attracted to animation in the first place.

The British industry operates in the shadow of the major US studios, such as Disney and Dreamworks, which finance big budget productions for global markets. Nor do British animators have the state support that has helped sustain larger companies in continental Europe. In an increasingly global market, Britain faces growing competition from animators in countries such as China, where "commodity" animation can be acquired cheaply.

The UK has traditionally excelled at high-quality, labour intensive animation – a craft process designed for the one-off special such as *The Wrong Trousers* or *The Snowman*. With the exception of Cosgrove Hall, the UK industry has not been geared up to produce either animation series – twenty or thirty shows at a time – or a feature-length film.

This primarily craft-based British industry is in the midst of far-reaching technological change, brought on by computer animation. This should lower production costs and so help expand the market for animation, but it also poses a challenge for companies based on traditional skills in drawing, model making and still-frame animation.

The industry's weakness is its limited ability to replicate and spread its products over larger markets, that could thus sustain larger companies and attract more investment. Distinctive know-how is vital to a knowledge-based business but it is not enough to sustain an ambitious, growing business. British animation has remained a cottage industry because it has lacked the complementary resources needed for growth: funds for investment, management expertise from outside the industry, skills in marketing and distribution.

Andrew McBean of ITEL, majority shareholders in Manchester-based Cosgrove Hall, explained the pressures on an industry that in his words is reaching a watershed. "We can make series animation for £170,000 per half hour. ITV will now pay £45,000-£50,000 per half-hour so you have to find a good two-thirds of the budget from somebody else. A distribution advance against a show is around £40,000. If you go to France you can get 35 per cent of the budget – a mixture of broadcast finance and money from CNC, the French state animation funder. So you might get, say, £60,000 from France. But that means some of the work will have to be done in France. You have two clients who both want to see scripts, storyboards etcetera. And you still only have £140,000 of your £170,000. So you need an outside equity investor to give you the final 20 per cent – he then wants some equity. And if you've done this deal with ITV through one of the broadcasters, they'll take equity as well. So you can end up as the producer, its taken you two years to make the show, you're taking say a 10 per cent fee (£17,000 in this case) and you may end up, if you're lucky with 20 per cent of the equity. It's pretty damn difficult. No animation company can succeed on its own. It's all about partnerships." Which is where the networks and clusters that sustain the industry come in.

How networks offset fragility

Animators see themselves as part of a creative community. Animation companies are often small, short-lived, sometimes coming together for one project and then disbanding. This fluid, small-scale structure promotes collaboration to fulfil the needs of large clients. Some 36 per cent of the companies surveyed by Skillset had experience of co-productions with other UK companies, while just over a quarter had been involved in international partnerships.

Compact clusters help sustain the industry because they promote collaboration on production. International networks however are also vital because they give access to partners, larger markets and new sources of money.

Networks tie together this small scale and fluid industry in four different ways:

- Networks are vital in rapidly sourcing freelance talent. Networks are vital for freelancers: their relationships with a small numbers of firms are often what keep them afloat, especially if they are working on projects of their own. These informal networks serve as sources of work, skills training and also sources of knowledge about grants, rights and royalties.
- Sub-contracting: animators, according to John Carey: "Help each other out an awful lot. A lot of subcontracting goes on and there is quite a lot of cross-fertilisation. We believe by sticking together we are probably better able to compete."
- Animation is small industry worldwide. UK animators are increasingly involved in international co-productions. Animation festivals and screenings are a regular part of the calendar. Most UK animators not only know each other and each other's work, but also are familiar with their colleagues overseas.
- The animation industry is concentrated around the media industry it serves. These networks provide ease of access to clients. The epicentre of the UK industry is in Soho, but it has several other

'pockets' of animation companies, most notably, Bristol, Cardiff and Manchester. These clusters were formed in slightly different ways, with different ingredients.

Customer-core clusters

The Soho and Cardiff clusters, in particular, have customers at their core. They are made up of many small companies, closely linked to the customers for their output: the advertising and media industry in London and S4C the Welsh language broadcaster in Cardiff.

Soho

Almost 60 per cent of companies and two-thirds of the workforce in the animation industry are based in Greater London. As Jerry Hibbert of Hibbert Ralph, based in D'Arblay Street Soho, puts it: "I can do pretty much everything I need to do in a few streets around here."

Physical proximity accounts for most of Soho's ability to act as a network. People, especially when young, tend to go drinking together after work and meet people from other companies. Proximity to customers is also critical. Hibbert Ralph and other animators work largely for the advertising industry that is also centred in Soho.

● *Soho case study: John Carey Films*

The offices of John Carey Films in a quiet street just north of Soho have been rented by a succession of animation companies since the 1960s. Like others in the business, Carey's sojourn there may also be limited – the studios were flat out working on the remaking of Captain Pugwash, but nobody could say what would happen after that. Carey is used to such levels of insecurity.

Carey's career is testimony to the resilience of the Soho animation cluster. His career has taken him through a succession of animation companies locally. Many of these folded after a brief period of success. Yet despite this turmoil, the cluster itself is still strong. The Soho cluster has provided Carey with near continuous employment for almost three decades.

Carey wanted to be in the film business from boyhood. His father composed music for films and his mother 'had something to do with the theatre.' At Westminster school he was lucky enough to be involved with an "arty crowd, I put plays on with the likes of Stephen Poliakoff and Nigel Planer." Even then he says, "we attacked doing school plays in a kind of professional way, took them on tour in the school holidays and so on. I got to the point where I thought, I really love this," but decided on film rather than the theatre as he was interested in the technical as well as the creative aspect of filmmaking.

"Much to my father's annoyance, I decided not to go to university, because I wasn't particularly academic" he says. He started as a messenger with an animation company in London at the start of the 1970s.

After three years freelancing he got his first 'proper' job in the cutting rooms at Halls and Batchelor where he developed the specialised skills of animation editing. When the firm folded, he moved to Richard Williams who at the time, "was regarded as the crème de la crème of animation studios." From there he moved to the BBC as an assistant editor, working on live action, drama and documentaries. Disillusioned by the BBC he moved back to Soho to complete his animation apprenticeship working on commercials.

After a couple of years he took the plunge and set up his own editing company. He rented a room in Wardour Street that his friends described as "a wardrobe". From there he started a company called Filmrights with two partners, which lasted seven years.

Carey was inspired by the example of David Puttnam, the creative producer of Chariots of Fire. Carey liked the combination of artistic work and running a business that producing implied. "I took to running a business quite naturally," he says. "I don't see a conflict between the artistic side and the business side of his work. I go back to the very old fashioned idea of a sort of filmmaker producer which had been around in the 1920s and 1930s."

The creativity comes from marrying creative work with the business discipline, he feels, especially with budgeting, "where you are working out what you can do for the money, what techniques will work best and so on. Where the money can be best spent to make a real impact on the audience."

Carey's most recent production was the remaking of animation classic, *Captain Pugwash*. It took him a couple of years of negotiation with Pugwash originator John Ryan to get the deal. Then he developed new scripts and a new approach to the animation and sent his ideas to broadcasters. The project was finally financed by the Britt Allcroft company, who had international success with *Thomas the Tank Engine*. Britt Allcroft is essentially a character licensing company. It financed the production of the series while retaining rights to exploit it on television and video, and through merchandising.

Carey accepts that animation is more difficult to finance than live action films, "because on the whole animation is for children and children's budget's tend to be smaller." And animation is expensive – roughly four times as expensive as a live action children's programme.

However the attraction is that animated films can have a very long shelf life. Carey edited *The Snowman* for Channel 4 in 1980: it is still shown every Christmas. "So the profile of animation is very different from live action TV in terms of finance. It tends to be a much longer burn, it tends to take longer to get the financing arranged and get the production together and once it is together the income steam comes in over a much longer period. It's kind of pension fund stuff."

Cardiff

The animation industry in South Wales started 1982, when S4C, the Welsh-language fourth station, was launched. It now includes several small and medium sized animation companies, including Ciriol and Cartwn Cymru. In the 1980s, S4C made animation series for children, including the successful *SuperTed*. Since then, it has moved on to commissioning more ambitious literary-based products, such as the series of animated Shakespeare's tales, Opervox, and most recently the Canterbury Tales.

Director of Animation Chris Grace at one stage had a budget of about £2.5 million per year to commission animation. The multiplier effects, through international partnerships for example, made that worth about £6 million.

Robin Lyons, of Ciriol, is critical of S4C's emphasis on Welsh language: "S4C is not interested in people who are independent. They are very hands on and act as producers rather than commissioners." Lyons says that for him the main advantage of being in Cardiff is that it is cheap. The local industry has built up a critical mass of skills which supports companies like Ciriol and post-production facilities have improved.

If the Cardiff animation cluster succeeds and prospers it will be largely due to the knock-on effect of S4C's determined and ambitious commissioning policy to build up a local supplier base and give it access to local and international markets.

Company-core clusters

While demand has been the honey-pot at the heart of the Cardiff and Soho clusters, the position in Bristol and Manchester is slightly different. In those cities, the initial demand for animation skills helped to create significant companies in UK terms, Cosgrove-Hall in Manchester and Aardman in Bristol, which both now act as important hubs in their own right within the cluster. That is not to say that other factors like demand, supply of talent and production facilities do not matter. They are of critical importance. It is simply that in these clusters two relatively large companies have emerged to provide added momentum for the cluster. The entrepreneurship that went into the formation of these companies has had a multiplier effect on the cluster as a whole.

Manchester

The Manchester network is a legacy of a single large company, Cosgrove Hall, the "animation factory of the north" as it describes itself.

Founders Mark Hall and Brian Cosgrove trained in graphic design and worked for Granada, the ITV broadcaster in the north-west. On leaving Granada, they set up a company together (StopFrame animation) on the basis of a contract to do an advertisement for the TV Times. That led to further advertising work and eventually Thames TV made a takeover bid. Cosgrove Hall became the sole provider of animation to the ITV network.

This was the heyday of vertical integration in TV companies – before independent producers came on the scene – and Cosgrove Hall grew to 150 people. It became one of the biggest animation companies in the world and was able to train its own talent.

When Thames TV lost its licence as a broadcaster to Carlton, Thames wanted to close the company down, retaining only Cosgrove and Hall and outsourcing all production. The distributor ITEL subsequently bought 75 per cent of the company that now operates as an independent producer. That Manchester still has a functioning animation industry is testament to Cosgrove Hall's success and its role in support-ing talent.

Bristol

The Bristol cluster, the most important in the UK outside London, got started in the 1970s when Dave Sproxton and Peter Lord, the founders of Aardman Animations, started making models for the BBC children's programme, *Vision On*, which was produced in Bristol. Aardman Animations is at the core of a network of Bristol animators. However, Colin Rose, head of animation at BBC Bristol, points out that the city in the 1970s was fertile ground for media industries, with BBC Bristol, a well-respected university drama department and the Bristol Old Vic. Animation benefited from theatre skills such as lighting and television skills such as camerawork.

The BBC played a critical role in getting the cluster going by commis-sioning early work. Rose was in charge of a BBC project to attract new film talent called *10 by 10*. This brought him into contact with the film schools and he realised there was a whole generation of animators who were making short films. Rose set up the BBC Animation Initiative in 1991, which led to the production of the Wallace and Gromit feature, *The Wrong Trousers*, among other successes.

The Bristol network is fairly self-contained. Rose explained: "You can do everything here: we have the full range of pre- and post-production down here." The Bristol network has emerged from a series of moves by commissioners, entrepreneurs, film schools and public policy makers, each building on the other but in a fairly ill-coordinated fashion. Julian Mellor of Bristol City Council commented: "Bristol is the second city for media in the UK. Forty per cent of world output of natural history programmes comes from Bristol. But that has come about more by accident than by design. We've discovered that we have a sleeping giant on our hands."

The Bristol network is informal, Rose explained: "It's tribal. It works because we all know each other. It's a collaborative cottage industry of small companies and freelancers. It does not need and could not be organised by large companies or institutions. The great success of the British animation industry is its individuality and creativity – it doesn't look like mass production."

However, at the centre of the Bristol cluster now stands Aardman Animation, the best known modern British animation studio. It attracts talent, work and investment to the local industry. Dave Sproxton is one of its founders.

● *Dave Sproxton, MD, Aardman Animations*
If the terms "animation" and "entrepreneur" don't always sit happily together in what is basically a cottage industry, then Dave Sproxton is the exception that proves the rule.

Sproxton started Aardman with a schoolfriend, Peter Lord. Both their fathers worked for the BBC, which helped "in that we had a camera in the cupboard," and also a contact in the BBC, Patrick Dowling, who was at that time producing the children's programme *Vision On*.

Sproxton and Lord had done some work for *Vision On* while they were still at school and after graduating (Dave in geography and Peter in English) they came to Bristol, as that was where *Vision On* and its follow up *Take Hart* was produced.

For a few years in the mid to late 1970s, they worked "hand to mouth", making animated inserts for children's programmes. Like many in animation, they were rescued from this relative obscurity by the arrival of Channel 4. A year before Channel 4 went on air, its then head Jeremy Isaacs held a party at the Cambridge Animation Festival to meet animators. Sproxton and Lord met him and, after sending him some of their material, were invited to meet the commissioning editor.

While at that meeting, the door opened and Isaacs put his head round that door and said, "I've just seen this five minute piece, can I have ten of them for the opening week of transmission?"

This was just eleven months before C4 launched. Lord and Sproxton didn't have the capacity to meet Isaac's request. So they offered him five shorts for the opening and five later. The series, which became the celebrated *Animated Conversations*, was delivered about six months late and went out in the week of Channel 4's first anniversary.

After the success of *Animated Conversations*, "the phone started to ring off the hook" from advertising agencies and "a world that we thought we would never get into" suddenly opened up. "We thought we'd be in and out of fashion in about six months," Sproxton confesses.

They viewed the chance to work on advertisements as an opportunity to make money to reinvest in the business. Commercial work is one way that they subsidise the research and writing of broadcast ideas. Aardman earns about £3.5 million a year from commercials, about half of which comes from the US, where they have developed the long-running Chevron campaign among others. As a result, Aardman has always being able to pay its way from existing work. Commercials still represent the backbone of their finances and have helped fund features like, *A Close Shave* (budget £1.2 million, of which Aardman put in 25 per cent). This also means they have not had to chase co-financing deals for broadcast material, as others in the industry have to do.

In 1985, Lord and Sproxton were joined by Nick Park who came from the National Film School. Park went on to create the famed Wallace and Gromit series, which won him an Oscar. The company's subsequent fame brought more interest from advertisers in what is a virtuous circle. It also helps develop the skills of staff members. "Broadly the arrangement is, you earn your keep on commercials and we will find both time and opportunity, a budget and a TV slot, for your own work," explains Sproxton. Aardman has a full-time staff of about 70 but has employed more than 100 freelancers when the company has been working on large projects.

Aardman has helped to create a pool of freelancers in the south-west and it has spun out a couple of small studios. When it started to prove difficult to recruit good animators the company helped set up the Bristol Animation Course at the University of the West of England (UWE) (see below).

Sproxton believes it has become harder for entrepreneurs starting a business on their own from scratch. The amount of regulation is "stacked against two guys in a bedroom." Once you get to Aardman's size, " you've got people to handle tax and National Insurance and that kind of thing, but for an individual, it's got tougher to deal with all the regulation." The kit for computer animation is getting cheaper but "you're not gonna compete with the big outfits in London 'cos the learning curve is still very steep." The loss of the "local bank manager" means that banks are less aware of what is going on in their area. "They're out to make money, not to help businesses grow. I think they're all thieves and brigands."

Given all this, he thinks it is unsurprising that the animation industry is not more entrepreneurial. "There are people in Aardman who could go off and do their own thing, but frankly, they're not going to, it's too much like hard work. It works for them here. They get more creativity out of their souls than they would do on their own. The creative industries, if they are driven by third party money, don't necessarily get the best out of people."

In addition, "the margins are so slender now" in TV work, he laments. Hence, for some of the smaller production companies, "it's a hobby, a lifestyle thing, not a business." In addition, holding on to rights and royalties is difficult. "We're lucky we've got a fair bit of clout" and now have very good, but expensive, media lawyers.

Sproxton never planned to go into business. He just wanted to make films. When he and Lord started out he admits they were naive about money. Channel 4 had to point out to them that they needed to add a mark up to costs to make a profit. "Then commercials came in, but still, we didn't regard it as a business and strangely, I still don't regard it as a business. It is a business but I'm not a businessman."

Does Sproxton see himself as an entrepreneur? "Probably. I like to do things differently, but not in the opportunist sense. I knew there was a value in what we did and if we liked it, then other people would too. Wallace and Grommitt is a good example: it is Nick's wonderful world. So we tend to be driven by our own ideas, if we enjoy them, the rest of the world will enjoy them."

"I'm not interested in making money for its own sake. What I'm interested in doing is creating stuff. My father was a producer with the BBC and we'd always been led to believe that the creative stuff was really what mattered in life. And we were led to believe that if you did what you believed in, you'd make a living out of it."

Aardman is run as a kind of creative community as much as a company. According to Sproxton it epitomises the industry: "It's a meeting of artists, rather than in a live action film festival, which is a meeting of commerce."

Prospects and policy

The British animation industry has several strengths: four relatively strong clusters; an international reputation for high-quality craft work;

a reasonably strong talent base fed by film and art schools; an established, albeit small, domestic market for its output through advertising and broadcasters. Moreover, the market for animation skills should expand with the growth of computer games and broadband communications, which will allow the distribution of much richer media content on the internet. Animation created using software such as Macromedia's Flash, is one of the growth content areas on the internet.

The structure of the British industry seems to be adapting to this new technology. Companies involved in digital and computer animation tend to be younger but as a result smaller than those in other sectors of animation. They are also likely to have a mix of skills and clients. Animation is only one part of their work, which also involves web design and internet technologies. Most of the industry's growth is expected to come from increased demand from websites and online advertising. Animation is a relatively young industry: about a quarter of the workforce has entered the industry since 1995. The average age in the Skillset survey was 34, with only 9 per cent aged 50 or more. The industry should have injections of new ideas and talent from people trained on new technologies.

Yet digitalisation will pose new challenges for an industry largely based on traditional tacit skills and know-how. Some in the industry expect production costs to be lowered, "Lots of studios have got in more computers," says Mark Taylor, who operates a small 2-D animation studio. "Computers speed up the work and can cut some costs by up to 70 per cent. We have two computer units, with operators doing the work of eight people."

However, computerisation will also allow more basic animation work to do done overseas. "A lot of work is going on in Mainland China at the moment," says Andrew McBean of ITEL, "because of wage rates. If the technology allowed that to happen but creative control to remain in the UK, for example, it may not cut costs, but it would raise the value of the work to the UK." The British industry's prospects, in other words, rest on its ability to innovate, by using new technology to build on its reputation for high-quality production.

Animation skills will be absorbed into other media – computer games, web design and interactive TV for example. A new generation of animation firms may emerge to exploit these opportunities but they will have to be multi-skilled in serving all these markets, rather than pure animation companies.

Many animators believe the industry needs active public policy to address the challenges it faces. They differ markedly on what kind of policy is required. Proposals to secure a market for local production through quotas or production subsidies are controversial even within the industry.

However there is a consensus that the industry needs closer links with further and higher education to make sure it can recruit the talent it needs. Small animation companies operate with tight margins and have little time for on the job training.

Animation training has been part of British art school education since the late 1960s. Clare Kitson, former commissioning editor for animation at Channel 4, believes this is one of the problems: "Animators in the UK are mostly trained at art schools, rather than film schools. So although they are creative, they are not necessarily technically aware nor good at narrative." Stuart Till of Polygram says the industry has "under-invested in training across the board." London, and Soho in particular, is home to many of the world's leading animation companies, but they have an acute problem finding recruits with the right combination of fine art and IT skills.

The long-term needs of the industry are only likely to be met by innovation in the way training is designed, delivered and funded. Out of necessity Aardman Animation in Bristol has developed a new course, the Bristol Animation Course, for animators with the University of the West of England. The post-graduate short course (six months) is aimed at people with some relevant experience who want to become animators. Initially, it was designed specifically to train puppet animators for Aardman's feature film *Chicken Run*, which was soaking up all the firms' skills and those of almost a hundred freelancers. Aardman initially provided the teaching and equipment for the course. Since then, UWE has developed a more general animation course, with help, both in money and in kind, from other firms in the Bristol animation community, including A for Animation. The companies provide tuition, placements, support and materials for the projects that form part of the instruction process. They also contribute to an Animation Training Fund that helps cover some of the £6,000 annual fees. Most of the students on the course are from continental Europe.

Sproxton says the course was set up because: "There is a fundamental shortfall between the expectation of students going to college to do animation and the ability of the colleges to deliver on that expectation and for the industry. The craft angle, I think, has been slightly denuded because of the change from polytechnics to universities. So the courses have become more research-driven and less, hands-on craft driven." The Bristol course is five days a week, eight hours a day and is designed to turn out immediately employable animators.

6. Knowledge entrepreneurship policies

It would be a mistake to over state the impact public policies can have on entrepreneurship and innovation. The most powerful forces driving entrepreneurship are:

- technological change and knowledge creation, which open opportunities for entrepreneurs to develop new products, services and organisations
- cultural change, which will make it more acceptable to take risks, work for yourself and start a business
- economic changes which will make working for large corporations less appealing and working for yourself more rewarding
- the willingness of financial markets and investors to sanction risk taking.

For a government that wants to promote entrepreneurship and innovation, the best policy would be to work with the grain of these changes.

Entrepreneurship has become so critical to the success of a modern economy, because it helps determine the rate at which new ideas are turned into new usable products and services. It cannot be left to chance. The entrepreneurial translation of ideas into businesses emerges from the way partnerships and teams are formed through the networks and clusters, which give entrepreneurs access to the other resources they need to build an organisation. Public policy can affect every aspect of this process, from the skills and capabilities of entrepreneurs, to the scale of the market opportunities they sense and the ease with which networks and clusters can develop.

We need a new infrastructure to support entrepreneurship. The industrial economy relied upon public and privately financed infrastructures of transport and energy, water and sanitation, factories and office buildings. An economy in which knowledge and innovation are driving growth needs a different infrastructure. Modern versions of old physical infrastructures, for transport and utilities, for example, still matter. Good international travel links are vital for any region that seeks to play a role in the global innovation networks that drive science, for example. The coverage and cost of new hard infrastructures of broadband telecommunications, computing and communications, will be critical.

However, alongside top-quality hard infrastructures a successful economy will increasingly need "soft" infrastructure to provide a platform for learning, creativity, entrepreneurship, innovation and business creation. The vital soft infrastructures include investment in education, skills and creativity; a formal knowledge-creating infrastructure of scientific research and cultural innovation; a financial infrastructure of business angels, incubators and venture capitalists that allows financial capital to be attracted to the best ideas and talent.

Over the past decade, the UK and many other countries have developed a raft of policies to widen access to capital, to speed business creation and to make it easier for universities to spin-off businesses. The task now is create a policy framework that is more coherent, systematic, comprehensive and inclusive, to promote entrepreneurship across society.

- A more systematic approach, because a widely spread capacity for entrepreneurship has become so vital to economic and social health. Entrepreneurs do not just create jobs and adjust to change. Entrepreneurship helps keep society open. Our entrepreneurial capacity cannot be left to the chance emergence of mavericks. We need to invest in it more systematically.
- A more comprehensive approach because entrepreneurship helps to create value in large and small organisations, public and private. Entrepreneurship is not just a business issue.

- A more coherent approach to draw together education, finance for business, knowledge transfer from universities, regional and cluster development, stock options and employee ownership. The ingredients of entrepreneurship policy are scattered across government. Entrepreneurship policy is not confined to tax and business regulation.
- A more inclusive approach to open up entrepreneurial opportunities and foster entrepreneurial networks in more depressed regions, in which the economic culture has been shaped by dependence on large manufacturing companies and where the rate of start-ups and business growth is relatively low.

Before describing some of the specific policies this new approach could embrace, we highlight two essential changes in the machinery of government policy.

The Knowledge Bank

The Knowledge Bank would be a largely publicly funded but mainly privately run organisation, that would become a critical player in the process of innovation and entrepreneurship. It would work in tandem with the small business service to increase the rate of business start up and growth, particularly among knowledge-based businesses. It would:

- Operate a time bank for managerial talent, donated by large companies and management consultancies, to work with small innovative companies. The Knowledge Bank would operate a brokering scheme to match companies to executive talent, either for permanent postings or for secondments.
- Promote local business clubs as the basis for clusters and networks, akin to the Cambridge Network or the First Tuesday initiative. The Knowledge Bank would fund intermediaries and facilitators whose goal would be to bring together entrepreneurs, larger companies, investors and business services companies, to strengthen creation infrastructure in a locality or city.
- Open a patent bank, into which large companies and universities could donate intellectual property that they did not know-how to exploit. Several large companies, such as Dow Chemicals, have

made "redundant" patents available to small business partners to exploit. Dow only protects a small proportion of its patent portfolio. The Knowledge Bank would operate an intellectual property sharing scheme across the UK corporate sector. A company that found one of its patents was being taken up could share in the proceeds.

- Incorporate the Patent Office, with the aim of turning it into an arm of industrial policy rather than simply an office that administers patents. The US Patent Office has played a critical role in promoting biotechnology. Similarly, the UK patent office could actively promote knowledge-based industries, were it clearly part of an organisation devoted to that goal.

- Provide access to the "angel-plus" level of finance that many growth companies find it hard to raise. Venture capital is an increasingly well-funded and well-organised industry in the UK, although still very concentrated in the south-east. Business angels, private investors who back very young companies, are also increasingly well organised, although they are nowhere near as well established as they are in the US. However, companies often experience a gap between angel investment, which usually goes no further than £500,000, and venture capital investment, which normally starts at more than £1 million. This gap often distorts a company's development. Either a company has to stay small because it cannot raise the finance, or – as in the case of Gremlin and Inner Workings – it leaps too far too fast to a more aggressive form of financing. The Knowledge Bank would help to fill in this missing step in the funding process by "topping-up" angel investments in high-risk new technology ventures. This would help companies to grow steadily.

- Promote the public sector's use of the products of innovative small companies. The Knowledge Bank would help open up the public sector market place to innovative companies, so that these companies could use the public sector's stamp of approval to seek markets elsewhere.

- Run a National Business Plan competition, a kind of Booker prize for business, in which school children, students and adult entrepreneurs could compete for prizes. The winners would receive proper financial support to take their plan forward. (Details of this are set out below.)

The creation of the Knowledge Bank should form part of a much wider reorganisation of the DTI to turn it into a much more effective agency for promoting entrepreneurship and innovation.

De-merging the DTI

Government restructuring will not dramatically increase entrepreneurial activity. Often, government restructuring turns into an elaborate and unproductive exercise in shuffling chairs. With those caveats in mind, it is also glaringly obvious that the machinery of government is extremely poorly adapted to the demands of an innovation-driven knowledge-based economy. There is a strong case for radical reform starting at the centre with the main business-oriented department: the Department of Trade and Industry.

The case for radical surgery at the DTI is very persuasive. The department resembles a 1970s conglomerate: an unwieldy assemblage of activities, gathered over a long period, often with little synergy or purpose.

The DTI combines separate departments that used to deal with trade and energy, as well as various industries that used to receive state support. Its activities are bewilderingly diverse. They range from industries such as aerospace and pharmaceuticals, dominated by large companies, in which the state plays a significant role through subsidies or price regulation, to industries such as information technology and electronics, which are newer and more entrepreneurial and where the state has a much more limited role. The department also attempts to bring together different, often incompatible, roles and cultures. One role is as a Whitehall policy maker covering a wide range of business related fields. A second is to help animate British business by delivering business support through publicly funded schemes. A third is as an independent arbiter of business regulations, for example, on company law and consumer legislation. A fourth is to act as an investor in its own right in the science base.

The outcome of this ill-coordinated clutter of activities and confusing roles is predictable. The department lacks a clear sense of purpose and rationale. It is constantly haunted by the shadow of the Treasury, which is the real master of economic policy and the Department for Education and Employment, which has a much bigger budget and a sense of real power.

The DTI suffers from a paucity of ambition and imagination: it runs scores of small, marginal schemes that generally involve only a few tens of millions of pounds. These schemes do little harm but as a result it is also difficult to measure the value they add. The DTI lacks any kind of dynamic, entrepreneurial and innovative drive. That may be defensible in its role as a policy-maker and regulator but not in its business support activities. In short the DTI, which employs about 9,000 people, is in dire need of a far-reaching shake-up.

The DTI should be de-merged into three distinct organisations, each focused on a specific role: policy, business support and regulation. In the process, over a long period of time, the number of people employed by the DTI should be significantly reduced. This is how the de-merger would work.

Policy making

The most important policy issues at the DTI revolve around how fiscal policy should be used to promote innovation, entrepreneurship and growth. Whenever the DTI comes up with a proposal for tax incentives for business it has to get Treasury approval. There is often huge duplication of effort in attempting to agree a common set of objectives and measures for policy. A more sensible approach would be to expand the Treasury's Innovation and Growth Unit to form an Enterprise Division at the Treasury that would take over most of the policy functions of the DTI and provide a much closer link between industrial and fiscal policy. Industrial and business thinking would be integrated into the heart of the Treasury rather than having to go via the much weaker DTI. The Treasury's Enterprise Division would oversee all fiscal policy making in relation to business.

In addition the Enterprise Division could house a cross-departmental Entrepreneurship Unit to examine the impact of different policies, enacted by different agencies and departments, on entrepreneurship. One possibility would be for this Entrepreneurship Unit to publish a series of entrepreneurship impact statements assessing the likely impact of regulations and policies on entrepreneurial capacity and opportunity. An alternative would be for these statements to be drawn up by a Select Committee of the House of Commons.

Sectoral policy issues – for instance covering coal subsidies or aerospace launch aid – could be covered by teams within the Treasury, combining industry experts drawn from the old DTI and fiscal policy experts from within the Treasury.

Three areas of policy making would not fall within the Enterprise Division. First, it would make sense to create a single policy making department to shadow Ofcom, the single regulator for broadcasting, communications and the media created by the 2001 Communications Bill. This could be achieved by integrating the DTI departments dealing with the media and communications into the activities of the Department of Culture Media and Sport thus making this small department more substantial. This would include oversight of the Post Office.

Second, the DTI's responsibility for employment legislation, training and industrial relations would pass to the larger Department for Education and Employment to allow it to develop a more integrated approach to education and training from school into work. In effect the DfEE would become the Ministry of Human Capital and Talent.

Third, the DTI's environmental work should become the business facing division of the environmental arm of the Department for Environment, Farming and Rural Affairs.

Even if this shake-up of policy-making functions is rejected, in part because it could centralise too much power in the Treasury, there is a powerful case for much tighter coordination between the Treasury and DTI on policy issues.

Business support

The DTI's business support activities should be taken out of Whitehall's bureaucratic, analytic and policy-making culture. Business support needs to be delivered in a far more dynamic, entrepreneurial, performance driven and business-like culture. All the schemes the DTI runs to help British business should be turned over to a Business Services Agency (BSA), which would be able to set new pay scales, attract talent from the private sector and create new methods of working.

The BSA would be the umbrella for five agencies, each focused on specific markets, needs and targets and run by management teams recruited for the task.

In addition to the Small Business Service and the Knowledge Bank, the BSA would include:

- The British Business Agency to handle inward investment and external trade promotion, including the Invest in Britain Bureau and the Trade Partners scheme.
- The Science and Innovation Agency would take in all the activities of the Office of Science and Technology as well as all the DTI's current spending on innovation. The Science and Innovation Agency would drive returns from investment in the science base through schemes such as University Challenge and Entrepreneurship Centres at universities.
- The Regional Economic Development Agency would take responsibility for coordinating the work of the Regional Development Authorities as well as the Regional Selective Assistance budget and all the DTI's local business support schemes such as Business Links.

The Business Regulation Agency
Policy making involves a keen sense of political priorities. Effective business support requires a business-like and performance-driven culture in which agencies can work very closely with their clients. Regulation on the other hand thrives in an atmosphere of rigorous independence. Regulators need to be able to stand back from the demands of politicians, producers and vested interests. That is why the DTI's regulatory responsibilities should be spun out into a new and politically independent Business Regulation Agency covering company law, mergers and acquisitions, consumer regulation and competition policy.

The DTI de-merger would not trigger a surge in entrepreneurial activity. However it would be a sign of the government's commitment to innovate to keep pace with change in the economy. The reorganisation would improve the quality and effectiveness of policy-making; make business support more focused and driven; and create a rigorously independent approach to business regulation, all of which would be useful.

A new framework for policy

A more systematic and coherent approach to entrepreneurship policy needs four main ingredients. It needs to:

- (i) Build up the supply side of the entrepreneurial economy: the entrepreneurial capacity and distinctive know-how needed to form knowledge-based businesses.
- (ii) Open up market opportunities through a market-creating competition policy, in the public as much as the private sector.
- (iii) Fund intermediaries, facilitators and networks to help mobilise resources around entrepreneurs.
- (iv) Promote entrepreneurship in regions and among groups of the population where entrepreneurship is less developed.

Responsibility for developing and pursuing this framework would rest with the Entrepreneurship Unit working within the Treasury's Enterprise Division. We briefly outline how policy might develop in each of these area.

(i) The supply side: entrepreneurial capacity

Britain needs a systematic policy to create a broadly spread capacity for entrepreneurship, starting with education and young people and extending to include older workers, mothers returning to work, family businesses and entrepreneurship among recent immigrants.

- *Basic education.* It will be near impossible to succeed in the knowledge-driven economy without high standards in the basics of literacy and numeracy across the entire population. But in a more entrepreneurial economy the content of education will have to change as well. Children in junior and secondary schools need to engage in creativity, problem-solving and teamwork, all key capabilities for the new economy. A much larger portion of the school curriculum needs to be devoted to focused, creative project work, in which children have to work flexibly in teams. As well as studying for exams a child should develop a sense of moving from project to project across their school career, building up skills and learning how to manage their own work and ideas.

Schools should be encouraged to experiment with different approaches to blur the lines between formal education, work experience and entrepreneurship. Possibilities include: allowing some small businesses that have educational aspects to their work – for example video production facilities – to rent space on school premises in exchange for providing kids with lessons; allowing schools to start their own small businesses, for example making computers for parents or providing services for local businesses.

- *Higher education.* Expanding access to higher education matters not just because young people may learn important skills but because they also learn independence, incubate ideas and form a more self-confident sense of themselves as autonomous individuals, all key ingredients in entrepreneurship. Education broadens people's horizons and encourages mobility. Universities can create an innovative atmosphere simply by bringing young people together. That is why university towns are often the spawning grounds for cultural businesses in fashion, design and music. There is growing interest in the formal teaching of entrepreneurship at universities. Seven Scottish universities offer modules in entrepreneurship to students in every faculty. In future every student should be able to opt-in to a course in entrepreneurship and self-employment, no matter what degree they are studying. In some disciplines, such as engineering and sciences, entrepreneurship modules, involving a good deal of practical work on business plan projects, should be compulsory.

- *Business education.* We need to create a much broader range of business qualifications and courses delivered by a wider range of institutions. Many people find the idea of sitting for a Masters in Business Administration daunting and expensive. One option would be to encourage the creation of Community Business Schools that could teach a range of short courses to people at work in a local business. Business skills are not the preserve of a managerial elite; they need to be spread far more widely in the population.

- *Attracting talent.* Britain needs to match the US as an attractive meeting place for entrepreneurial talent from around the world.

The cream of the mobile, educated young global workforce is being attracted to the US and the West Coast in particular, not just because the rewards are so lucrative but because US society is in many ways more open and cosmopolitan. In a knowledge economy, in which human capital and talent are critical, immigration policy needs to be seen, in part, as an arm of industrial policy. One measurable aim of policy should be to target and attract internationally mobile talent in key sectors of the economy to strengthen Britain's position in areas like mobile telecommunications and biotechnology.

Successful businesses are built on distinctive know-how. We need to invest more in research and development, both in universities and companies, and generate a higher return from that investment. Investment in the science base, both public and private, needs to be matched by measures to ease the flow of ideas into the rest of the economy. Measures such as the University Challenge Fund, the creation of Entrepreneurship Centres and the links the government is helping to forge between universities and large businesses need to be spread to many more universities, especially in areas of relative economic deprivation.

Valuable distinctive knowledge is often not formal, scientific or technical but creative, cultural and craft based. Cookery, design, music, film, fashion and games are increasingly important parts of the economy. Education needs to pay greater attention to building creative and craft skills, for example, through specialist schools and curricula.

(ii) Opportunities for entrepreneurs

One theme of policy should be to enhance people's capacity to sense and then articulate opportunities. Business plan competitions, in which people of all ages can conceive and develop ideas, should become a national pastime. Only through practical work on projects that matter to them will people develop skills to seek, scan and select promising opportunities.

Many young people might be inspired to start their own business by exposure to successful older entrepreneurs. One possibility would be to run a Entrepreneurship Scholarship Programme for eighteen to 21 year olds to allow them to develop an idea for a business by visiting the US or by working alongside a successful British-based entrepreneur.

Markets that are open to new entrants with new ideas will encourage people to see new opportunities. If markets are closed to new entrants by regulation or monopoly power then there will be only a limited sense of opportunity. The case for a rigorous competition policy to promote new entrants is not that deregulation lowers costs for consumers but that it enhances opportunities for entrepreneurship. The need for tough competition policy applies as much to services, professions and the public sector as to traditional industrial sectors. In the public sector, the goal should be to open opportunities for new entrants thus making public sector markets far more contestable. The threat that a new entrant might come in with a much better way to deliver the council tax or a better way to offer patients hospital appointments should help spur public sector incumbents to improve their performance.

Larger markets tend to breed larger opportunities. In the US a company that has a hit in its domestic market is likely to have a very large hit. Success in the US market so often can be the basis for international expansion. In Europe, despite the single market programme and moves towards harmonisation, markets are often still nationally defined. As a result entrepreneurs see smaller opportunities and build smaller businesses.

Entrepreneurs are not just good at sensing an opportunity, they can assess and articulate its potential to investors and partners who might back the project. Central to this is the skill of creating and presenting a business plan. These skills should become widely spread through basic education. Writing business plans should become a national pastime. To promote it the government, with the backing of venture capitalists and the investment community, should create a National Business Plan competition – a kind of Booker prize for entrepreneurs. The National Business Plan competition would operate annual regional competitions run by Regional Development Authorities with categories for school children, students and adult entrepreneurs, including prizes for entrepreneurs over the age of 50 and women. The winners of the regional competitions would go forward to a national final. The national final winners would be given support to take their plan forward. The

National Business Plan competition would be a vast annual showcase for entrepreneurial talent and ideas, which would not just highlight the value of entrepreneurship but also in the process create a string of real businesses and jobs.

(iii) Mobilising resources

● *Networks and clusters*
Modern entrepreneurs are sustained by networks and clusters. Can policy-makers help to promote an innovative capacity within clusters, to give them a life, possibly stretching over several waves of technology?

The answer is yes, but only if public policy is designed intelligently. Clusters and networks, when they work well, are too fluid to be amenable to direct public management. However clusters need "public goods" to sustain them: shared infrastructure, facilities, resources, meeting places. There is a role for third parties, intermediaries, brokers, facilitators and networkers who help to make links between different companies and bring them together. One role for public policy is to make sure this kind of networking and bridge building takes place. That does not mean public bodies should undertake this role; simply that they could fund or facilitate it. Clusters which lack such intermediaries or "collective resources for competition" may be held back. While some of these shared resources can be created by private companies, for example galleries and bars, some resources, such as finance and work-space, might require more concerted policy focus.

Different clusters have different needs. No single set of policy tools is applicable to all clusters. Science-based clusters, for example, are relatively amenable to direct public policy interventions through invest-ment in the scientific knowledge base, the creation of science parks and schemes to transfer knowledge out of universities into nearby compa-nies. Technology clusters, like the Thames Valley corridor that rely heavily on large multinational companies can be promoted partly by inward investment schemes to attract global software companies and the provision of a sound infrastructure. However clusters such as the Hoxton new media triangle in London, which are not based on insti-tutions, formal knowledge or large companies, are far less amenable to direct policy intervention. In Hoxton the lack of direct policy was a critical factor in the area's growth.

Different policies are needed at different stages of a cluster's development. At the early stages a cluster is more likely to grow if companies with similar skills and markets can be brought together to generate momentum. However, as a cluster develops its continued growth will depend on diversifying the kinds of companies in the area, to bring in new ideas, talent and technologies.

Culture matters as much if not more than infrastructure and institutions. Dynamic clusters need an entrepreneurial, expansive, risk-taking culture in which new firms are being created and large companies are spinning out smaller companies. All clusters need entrepreneurial role models and success stories to motivate those who follow, as well as access to appropriate kinds of finance and venture advice to help build businesses.

Clusters cannot be promoted from Whitehall. They can only be nurtured very close to the ground. This is one reason why many DTI responsibilities for business support need to be devolved to regions and cities.

Those cluster creating policies should include:

- Creating business incubators in most cities and major towns, to provide companies with managed workspace and easy access to a range of business services, accountants, legal services, management and marketing expertise. In the US young businesses are supported by a much larger and broader base of business angel investors. Incubators can play a critical role to make good the relative weakness of angel investors in the UK. Every significant town and university in the UK should have at least one business incubator within the next five years.
- Promoting peer-to-peer learning and clubs among entrepreneurs to help them develop projects. Although the First Tuesday business club has passed its peak, these clubs are still very popular and more are being created. These clubs might be focused around a set of disciplines: for example, a cultural entrepreneurs club has been created at the Institute of Contemporary Arts in London and a sister club is being founded in Glasgow. The Scottish Games Alliance is still

thriving and has helped to spawn TIGA, The Independent Games Alliance across the UK.

● *Finance*
(i) Micro-funding The family will be an important source of entrepreneurial finance. Many small businesses in the UK start around a kitchen table or in a bedroom. In the US many small businesses start with an initial investment from a close relative. One possibility would be to give tax advantages for one family member to invest in a business being created by another. This might particularly help ethnic minority businesses which are more likely to rely upon informal and familial sources of capital. A further idea would be to introduce a nil-rate tax band for micro-business run from home in the first two years of their life when they are most vulnerable to cashflow problems.

(ii) Angel-plus finance The Knowledge Bank would fill the "angel plus" gap in financing growth companies. However the absence of debt finance for high-tech and knowledge-based businesses means they are heavily dependent upon equity investment from venture capitalists. US banks, in contrast, have innovated a range of new products to allow them to lend to high-tech companies. In the UK only HSBC has a dedicated national high-tech lending team. British banks should be encouraged to learn lessons from the US experience.

(iii) Venture capital Venture capital should become a mainstream activity. Government measures outlined in the Myners Report on financial markets and pension funds should lead to significantly higher investment by pension funds in venture capital funds. That in turn should allow funds to be larger, develop more diversified portfolios and take a longer-term view on their investments. A genuinely European venture capital industry will develop only with a single, larger financial market that will allow investors to diversify risks.

One of the biggest constraints on growth businesses is the dearth of effective managerial talent to work alongside young entrepreneurs. Three initiatives would help to overcome this problem. The Knowledge Bank would act as a broker, bringing together managers from large companies and small companies that needed their expertise. Policy changes could make it more attractive for an experienced executive to join a start-up. Although British stock option laws have been relaxed they are still considerably more onerous and complicated than in the US, in large part to prevent their abuse by executives of large companies. We should make it easier for large companies to "lease" out managers to smaller companies. This "lend-lease" scheme for managerial talent would allow large companies to give managers an opportunity to join a start-up for up to two years without losing the executive altogether.

(iv) An inclusive approach

Entrepreneurship policy must not be designed simply for an entrepreneurial elite, many of whom probably have skills, contacts and money of their own to start a business. Policy should be designed to promote entrepreneurship across all sectors of society. It should be inclusive, socially and regionally.

● *Social promotion of entrepreneurship*
Entrepreneurs tend to be aged 25 to 44 years old. The larger the share of the population in this age group, the more entrepreneurs a society is likely to create. An ageing society faces particular problems in promoting entrepreneurship. This is an area where novel public policy approaches could pay dividends, for instance to create business clubs for entrepreneurs who are more than 50 years old. Increasing the participation rate of people over the age of 50 in entrepreneurship should be one measurable target of policy.

Entrepreneurs tend to be male. To expand the population of entrepreneurs, British programmes must get more women involved, which means attacking the prejudices that make it especially difficult for women to form their own businesses. (UK women start around half the number of businesses of an equivalent number of US women.) The government should launch a series of initiatives aimed at increasing markedly the participation rate of women in entrepreneurship. One possibility would be to launch programmes modelled on the Wellpark programme in Scotland which offers dedicated facilities with low rents, and on site childcare for women entrepreneurs.

● *Regions*

Entrepreneurship is heavily biased towards the south-east of the UK where the majority of businesses are created. That is in part because the south-east is the richest regional economy and the centre for venture funding. Government policy should focus wherever possible on building up the entrepreneurial capacity of other regions where dependence upon manufacturing industries and large companies has been one factor in limiting entrepreneurial activity. The government sponsored regional venture capital funds will start to redress the balance but further measures will be needed to make it easier for businesses to raise money from the region where they are based. Policies to promote clusters and networks should be biased towards regions with relatively low rates of business start-up.

Appendix
Main companies and entrepreneurs interviewed

Robin Saxby, Chief Executive, ARM
ARM is one of the most successful high-tech companies ever created in the UK. A spin off from Acorn Computers, ARM designs the low-energy consumption core to semi-conductors that are mainly used in mobile telephones. By 2001, about eight years after is foundation, ARM was the biggest semi-conductor maker in the world.

Edwin Moses, Chief Executive, Oxford Asymmetry
Oxford Asymmetry specialises in making complex compounds for research by pharmaceuticals companies. Moses joined when the company had only a handful of employees. In the course of the study the company was sold to Evolve, a German biotech group for more than £300 million.

Paul Drayson, Chief Executive, PowderJect
Powerject has patented a new technique for delivering medicines in powder form which removes the need for an injection. The technique was invented by Professor Brian Bellhouse from Oxford University.

Andrew Rickman, Chief Executive, Bookham Technologies
Bookham makes optical components for telecommunications switches to enhance their ability to transmit high speed data. At one stage worth more than $1 billion, the company was worth more than $500 million at the start of 2001.

Danny Chapchal, Cambridge Display Technologies
CDT was founded by Cambridge University Profressor Richard Friend, to exploit his discovery that light-emitting plastic could be used to make thin flat screens. Danny Chapchal was chief executive in 1998-99.

Peter Florence, Radioscape
Radioscape is one of Britain's most prolific radio technology companies. It has developed a wide range of tools and products to speed the development of software defined, digital radio that could not only widen use of digital radio but also provide a competitor to new generations of mobile telephone.

Brent Hooberman, LastMinute.com
Lastminute.com was synonymous with the dot.com boom of the late 1990s. The firm started by Hooberman and his colleague Martha Lane Fox was floated on the London Stock Market in early 2000 on a wave of publicity only to see its share price slump.

Tony Rowland and Robert Norton, ClickMango
ClickMango, the alternative health site, was one of the early casualties of the dot.com crash.

Tim Carrigan, NoHo Digital
NoHo Digital was one of London's first fully fledged multimedia production companies, which started through a partnership between Carrigan, a former journalist and a creative team from the BBC. It survived through a series of financial booms and slumps before being sold to WPP, the advertising agency.

Rowan Douglas, WIRE
Rowan Douglas was 23 when he created WIRE in 1994 to deliver information from the internet to insurance and reinsurance companies. WIRE subsequently developed a series of insurance products and trading systems before it was sold to one of the world's leading insurance brokers, Willis, in late 2000. Douglas and his executive team joined Willis to develop WIRE within its overall e-business strategy.

Roy Stringer, Creative Director, Amaze

Amaze is a leading internet and distance learning systems design company based in Liverpool. Amaze was created on the basis of technology developed at Liverpool University.

Steven Bowbrick, Funmail/Another.com

Steve Bowbrick founded WebMedia which in the mid-1990s was London's leading web design and services company. WebMedia was such an early web pioneer that it went bust before the dot.com wave had even appeared. Bowbrick went on to form Funmail with his backer Joel Kerner.

Nick Denton, Chief Executive, Moreover

Denton is a former FT journalist who formed Moreover with software specialist Angus Banks in 1997-98. Moreover was originally conceived as a tool for users to create their own internet news services but it has since become a business intelligence tool.

Daljit Singh, Creative Director, Digit

Daljit Singh created Digit with his business partner Andy Chambers after leaving IBM. Digit has since gone on to become one of London's leading web design companies, winning Design of the Year award from Design Magazine.

Simon Waterfall, Creative Director, Deepend

Simon Waterfall created Deepend with some colleagues from the Royal College of Art in the mid-1990s. Waterfall is the creative director while Gary Lockwood provides the business drive behind the business. Deepend has offices in seven countries.

Jez San, Founder, Argonaut Software

Jez San wrote his first hit computer game in his bedroom while still at school. He went on to create Argonaut Software, one of the UK's most successful games developers. In the process San also created ARC, which designs semi-conductors for games consoles. ARC was spun off as a separate business and listed on the stock market.

Dave Sproxton, Managing Director, Aardman Animations
Dave Sproxton was one of the founders of Aardman Animations, whic
has become of the most successful animation companies in the UK in
recent times, making Chicken Run and the Wallace and Gromit series.

Jerry Hibbert, Hibbert Ralph Animation
Hibbert Ralph is one of the longest established British animation
companies with a base in London's Soho.

John Carey, John Carey Films
John Carey, also based in Soho, is one of the most successful British
animators over the last two decades.

Peter Molyneux, Founder, Lionhead Studios
Molyneux is one of Britain's most successful computer games entrepreneurs. An early game of his, Populous, became one of the most
successful games of all time. His first games company, Bullfrog, was sold
to Infogrames of France. He went on to start a new company, Lionhead,
to make a new generation of computer games such as Black & White.

Lesley Keen, Inner Workings
Lesley Keen was one of the few successful women entrepreneurs in the
games and multimedia business. However, in the course of this study
Inner Workings folded after running out of money for further games
development.

Chris van der Kuyl, VIS Interactive
Chris van der Kuyl is one of the best known and most ambitious
computer games entrepreneurs in Scotland and with others has been
responsible for building up a games cluster in Dundee and Dunfermline.